Stop Fighting, Start Living
Unraveling Temptation

by Vernon Terrell

ISBN: 9781704770970

Download your free Battle Blueprint diagram at:
https://StopFightingStartLiving.com

The website also has more information on our leader training portal available for purchase (a full, done-for-you training experience with teaching videos corresponding to each session for yourself and / or small group).

DEDICATION

To Dr. Geoffrey "Grat" Correll, MD who used his incredible artistic skills as a teenager to design the very first Battle Blueprint illustration...you brought my vision to life in such a beautiful way. I have tweaked and changed a few things over the last 30+ years but the basic design is the same. Thank-you.

To my kids...you guys are amazing. I appreciate all your support as we faced so many trials and temptations together as a family. I could not ask for a better crew to help me navigate this awesome adventure we call life.

To my wonderful friend Daniel Harper, who showed me the value of friendship and keeping things in the light. You, Becca and your entire family are an inspiration to me and so many others.

To David and Anne Harper, your example inspires me to continue learning and growing in my faith. Helping you with your book inspired me to finish mine, and for that I am so grateful.

To my Browns Bridge Church family, especially my InsideOut and globalX friends (yes, that includes all you Merida Amigos), you have already make a difference in my life. Serving with you to love and encourage others is what life is all about.

To the Lion Life Community, specifically Brody and Amy, and all those officers and inmates at the Cherokee County Adult Detention Center, it has been a privilege sharing the "truth that sets us free" and serving alongside you.

To Mike Quarles, my webinar partner, mentor and friend. I have learned so much just serving and doing life with you. Thanks.

...seriously, don't skip this part!

Why am I writing this book and what's in it for you? First, this book has been in the making for a very long time or perhaps, my understanding has been in a slow-cook crock-pot and is just now about ready to share. For years I believed I must fight this battle of temptation and overcome sin in my life to experience the victorious life in Christ. I knew all too well my own shortcomings and felt like such a hypocrite if I dared encourage or support others while secretly failing to win the sin battle in my own life.

Don't get me wrong, there are sound Biblical principles, guidelines, warnings, encouragement, exhortations, strategies and more to bolster our human frailties BUT they are NOT the answer to the real problem. Defining the problem correctly is the first step. So what is your problem?

Do you struggle with lust, lying, greed, deceit, porn, pride, drinking, drugs, sex, sugar, food, anger or hate? Just pick one. Is that your problem or one of your problems? The next obvious question is how do we fix it, stop it, or correct it, right? We look in the scripture and find verses to address the issue or issues and begin our journey to achieve victory over the sin that so easily knocks us down...and often it works. We see some light at the end of that dark tunnel. We begin to feel good about ourselves; our hypocrisy levels are down when we love, serve and minister to others. Our secret behavior begins to align with our outward behavior...we are victorious and free, or so we think.

And then it comes out of nowhere. Another temptation driving us toward the behavior we so desperately want to avoid. We try to fight it but for some reason we just give in, like we don't even care, and there we are again...defeated. Our streak of "victory" is now broken, we're back to square 1 (or square 0 for some). Does that sound familiar? If so, I totally understand. That was me for so many years. I am writing this book to share a few things I learned in my journey of faith, especially around the topic of temptation.

So what's in it for you? My hope is that you will simply take one step closer knowing Christ as your Life. Yes, I will share some insights on the process of temptation, the tempters and a few strategies along the way BUT my real hope is that you experience a paradigm shift on how you view "the battle" and how you define "victory". I want you to let go of your reputation and learn to experience life. I want you to STOP fighting and START living. I know, it may sound like you're giving up, or not giving it your best, but ask yourself this question...how's your current strategy working for you? If it's working well, pass this book along to someone else OR keep it should your tried and true strategy break down at some point.

I edited a poem I wrote years ago, you'll notice some of the old KJV (King James Version) verbiage, that provides a glimpse of where we are headed. I hope you enjoy.

Miracle
I long to be a miracle to everyone I see,
for Thou, O Lord, can verily make a miracle out of me.
My flesh doth strive and tries to quench Thy mighty working power,
so to the cross you lead me to remind me of the hour.

"It is finished!" You cried that glorious day You died upon the tree,
so too my striving ended when in Christ I died with Thee.
A new creation, holy and pure is what I am today,
forgiven, loved, accepted and complete in every way.

No longer is it I but Christ; He's won the victory!
The battle was never mine to fight but Christ Who lives in me.
Surrendered, now, to Your Life within and trusting You by faith,
the Life of Christ is manifest, a miracle of Your grace.

by Vernon Terrell

Great News! 1

Are you connected?

Let's begin with the most important question of your life…are you connected to God? I'm not referring to your church attendance, giving habits, social morality or anything similar. If God is truly the creator of the universe and if Jesus is God, as demonstrated by pulling off the most talked about event in history, His own resurrection from the dead, then connecting with God through Christ is a no-brainer for those who want to experience a "resurrection" type of power in their own life. For the Christian, power and victory rest in the finished work of Christ on the cross. Are you connected to His incredible power through Christ? If not, this book may be a good read, but it will not really make any meaningful impact on your daily experience. If you're interested, let's take a look at one illustration the Master Teacher (Jesus) used to describe connecting with God, and once and for all make sure YOU are connected!

In the New Testament book of John 15:1-5 Jesus creates a picture of connecting with God saying,

"I am the true vine, and My Father is the vine-dresser. Every branch in Me that does not bear fruit, He takes away; and every branch that bears fruit, He prunes it so that it may bear more fruit. You are already clean because of the word which I have spoken to you. Abide in Me, and I in you. As the branch cannot bear fruit of itself unless it abides in the vine, so neither can you unless you abide in Me. I am the vine, you are the branches; he who abides in Me and I in him, he bears much fruit, for apart from Me you can do nothing."

Do you see the picture? Let's start with the job responsibilities in this illustration. First, Jesus is the vine and not just any vine but the "true vine". There are plenty of vines out there offering all kinds of promises but none of those can impart Life…true, genuine life that can only come from the Creator of life.

The second role of vine-dresser is the responsibility of the Father. How many times do we (or other well-meaning Christians) jump head first into the role of vine-dresser? The vine-dresser tends to the vine, branches and the fruit yet often we feel it necessary to play fruit inspector in our own life and for some, in the lives of others. We judge the quality and quantity of fruit and even make calls on who is or is not in the Vine. Heads up folks, not our job! All that stuff is in the very capable hands of the Father.

Our job as a branch is very simple, we are told to abide in the vine. That's it. And there's nothing that fancy about the word abide, it simply means to remain, dwell, or live. As a branch, we draw life from the vine. Sometimes the branch may get tangled up or buried in the dirt and simply not bear fruit yet it is in the vine! I admit I have, at times, had my head in the dirt and chased after so many things this human life offers only to miss the real life that comes from Christ. The vine-dresser may need to *"airo"* or take away, lift or raise up (and sometimes shake off the dirt) so we can be in a position to bear fruit. He may need to cut-away or prune part of the branch to bear more fruit. The point being, you can only bear fruit when you are connected to the vine; if you are not connected, you simply dry up and wither away. Of course, that begs the question, how do I abide in the vine? How do I connect?

Throughout the gospel of John that question is answered over and over and over again. Believe. Believe that Jesus Christ is who He said He is...God in the flesh who came to earth not to show us how to perform better for God, but to pay the penalty of sin and death for all mankind so we could connect with God. Jesus told His crew in John 14:1, "Do not let your heart be troubled; believe in God, believe also in Me" and in the most famous verse in the Bible, John 3:16, "For God so loved the world, that He gave His only begotten Son, that whoever believes in Him shall not perish, but have eternal life."

ALL THOSE WHO BELIEVE ARE ABIDING IN THE LIFE OF CHRIST!

Believing is simply trusting that Christ sacrifice on the cross is sufficient payment for your sin problem, and through faith receive His forgiveness and new life. All those who believe ARE abiding in the life of Christ.

"You do not have His word abiding in you, for you do not believe Him whom He sent" -John. 5:38.

So, we come back to the most important question of your life, are you connected to God? Would you like to be connected? If you need a little help, I have written a prayer that you can pray that might express the desire and belief in your heart. The prayer itself is not a sentence with magic words…words are words. Jesus did not say recite these words, He said believe. The prayer below is simply a way to express that belief back to God.

―――――――――――――――――――――――――――――

"Jesus, I believe you are God, that you died on the cross and rose again to pay for MY sin. I know I don't understand it all, but right now I receive your free gift of forgiveness and eternal life. Help me to understand and grow more in my new faith. Thanks so much. Amen"

―――――――――――――――――――――――――――――

If you prayed that prayer for the first time, drop me a note at vterrell@FreeNHim.org. If you are already (or just now) a "believer" in Christ, remember our role…we are branches! Branches have one primary job, to abide, and after believing you are abiding right now…relax.

Don't make abiding a work to perform; you don't see branches in the field struggling and straining to produce fruit and neither should you. In fact, John 15 never tells us to "produce fruit". The vine does all the producing and the branch "bears fruit". As we continue in this book you will find some very similar ideas; spoiler alert…we don't produce victory either. There is so much to discover, so let's get going.

The war is already won!

What? The war is already won? Seriously? Are you living on the same planet as I am? I know, we all struggle (myself especially). Our struggle, however, does not invalidate the truth that Christ conquered sin and death through His death, burial and resurrection. The war IS over but the struggle while on this earth and in this body remains.

"For indeed while we are in this tent, we groan, being burdened, because we do not want to be unclothed but to be clothed, so that what is mortal will be swallowed up by life" -2 Corinthians 5:4

What is YOUR struggle? Is it your pride? Perhaps your words just don't come out the way you want them to? Is it pornography, lust or other sexual issues? What about anger, hate, fear, anxiety, or depression? Do you struggle with addictive behaviors like alcohol, drugs, food, or something else? Do you have that "something" that seems to always get the best of you? Don't worry, you are NOT alone (I know, not necessarily a lot of comfort in that statement). If you didn't struggle with something I might doubt your humanity (Vorlon or Vulcan perhaps? -reference to the Sci-Fi shows Babylon 5 and Star Trek for the truly enlightened).

WE ARE ALL TEMPTED, AND AT TIMES WE ALL FAIL

I remember when I found my first Playboy magazine around age 14 (yes, I was born before the internet existed)…I thought I was in heaven until later realized the fire and fury that comes with pornography. So glad I am free from that stuff (which, by the way, does NOT mean I am free from temptation or always experience victory, but by God's grace

I do experience His victory a lot more than I used to). At 15 years old I accepted Christ as my Savior and jumped-in headlong into knowing God and sharing Christ with others…but the struggle remained. God did not "ZAP" me and remove all sexual temptation and sexual desire from my body (kinda glad He did not, I do have 3 awesome kids that came the old fashion way with my awesome wife, but I digress).

YOUR LIFE SHOULD NOT BE CENTERED AROUND YOUR STRUGGLE, BUT RATHER HIS VICTORY

The point is we are ALL tempted, and at times we all fail. That's not an excuse, it is simply a reality of our human condition. And what is temptation anyway? Do we even understand the process? How do we deal with temptation once we are in the middle of it? Where is God in all of this?

Well, in this book I hope to answer or at least provide some insight to these and other questions. There is a danger, however, in my writing and you reading this book. Together we are focused on this topic of temptation, the struggle and tension we all deal on a consistent basis BUT the Christian life should NOT be centered around our struggle with temptation but rather on the finished work of Christ on the cross. The enemy of our souls would like nothing more than for you and I to focus on our temptation and struggle. Be aware of the danger.

Have you noticed in life that where you focus is where you tend to go? Like when my dad began teaching me to drive he made one request, "don't hit the mailboxes". Well, as a new driver, my focus immediately was not on driving anymore but rather on NOT hitting the mailboxes as I drove. Guess what, I won the prize for the youngest driver to barely miss every mailbox on my street…my father never drove with me again in my teen years, it was that terrifying.

When I hit my mid-40s I had a mid-life crises of sorts…I wanted a motorcycle! I took the safety and training courses and got my 2006 Yamaha FJR1300. What a beautiful bike! One thing we learned in my training was "where you look, there you will go". When you are on two wheels, the very weight distribution of your body effects your ride. If you "lean left", you tend to go in that direction and if you focus your eyes in one direction, your body and the bike tend to follow. We were taught when navigating a steep curve not to look at what you need to avoid hitting, instead focus on where you want to go and the bike, generally, will follow.

God wants you to drive (or ride), not focus on NOT having an accident. Yes, be wise, drive safe, be smart, but driving is about driving. Enjoy the ride. If you spend your life trying so hard not to fail you will not experience the joy of living. Christ has come to give you life, and life more abundant than you can imagine! And guess what, in the coming chapters I will let you in on a few insights that may just blow your mind - insights around forgiveness, victory, and even the mystery hidden from the foundation of the world! As my Pastor always says…you've got to read your Bible or you're missing out on some really cool stuff.

REFOCUS! STOP TRYING TO AVOID THE ACCIDENT AND SIMPLY ENJOY THE RIDE

As I mentioned, one thing to know about me is that I often think in diagrams, pictures, graphics, and flow charts. The foundation of this book is one diagram that I actually created in the early 1980s, The Battle Blueprint. As a Youth Director in the 1980s, I introduced this idea to students. One student, who was an incredible gifted artist, actually created my first Battle Blueprint diagram from a basic design I provided. I bet I still have that "original" today…it was very cool. I really struggled with temptation and wanted to understand what was going on and how to fix it! It took many years to understand the "fix" had already happened! Now before we jump into the diagram itself, let's go back to the original statement I started with in this chapter. Is the war actually over?

What "war" are we referring to? Yes, that is the question of the day! We're not referring to a physical war between nations nor are we referring to a war for social justice or some higher moral standard. When Jesus showed up on planet earth women and children were substandard humans, slavery was alive and well, and poverty, illiteracy and elitism was rampant, but those travesties of justice were not what Christ came to battle. The stakes were much higher if you can believe it. Mankind was lost to sin and death after the fall of Adam and Eve...the battle was against sin and death, a battle that no mere man had any hope of winning, but Jesus is no mere man. He is the incarnation of God Himself...God in human flesh living among us.

The enemy of our souls tried, as he did with Adam and Eve before, to lie and deceive our Savior but to no avail. The battle was always headed to the final showdown, the cross. The cross represented a most brutal death but to defeat sin and death, Jesus had to die in the most cruel and shameful manner. Death, however, could not hold the Son of the Living God. Jesus' resurrection obliterated death. Jesus, the One who lived without sin, won back the human race, "for the wages of sin is death, but the free gift of God is eternal life in Christ Jesus our Lord" -Romans 6:23. Yes, the infinite God paid the full price of sin and shame for finite man and says to you and I,

"...that whoever believes in Him shall not perish, but have eternal life" -John 3:16.

15

The war is over. John 19:30 tells us

"therefore when Jesus had received the sour wine, He said, 'It is finished!' And He bowed His head and gave up His spirit."

It REALLY is finished. Done. Over. Sin and death have been overcome by forgiveness and life. The Battle Blueprint is not really about how to fight sin (Jesus already won that battle), but how to recognize and unravel the lies that tempt us and lead us to sin. You are ALREADY victorious because of Christ, but are you experiencing that victory in your life? If not, the first place to start is understanding how the cross actually changed you once you believed. It's quite amazing.

Questions

Explain the different "job descriptions" as illustrated in John 15:1-5?

Are you connected? Briefly describe how you connected with God?

Describe a time in your life where trying NOT to do something (or trying to avoid "sin") was counter-productive.

As best you can, what does John 19:30 mean to you and how does that impact your life?

2

Freedom Rings

Understanding my identity

What happens when a person accepts Christ as Savior, when they believe, receive, call, or repent (don't get caught up with that word, it simply means to change the mind or consider again; basically, from not believing to believing)? This may blow your mind (or some of your theology) so hang on tight.

For hundreds of years before Christ, beginning with Socrates and continuing with Plato and Aristotle, many believed man was simply comprised of a body and soul - a two-part being; reason was catapulted to the top of the enlightenment food chain. But is that all there is? What about in the very beginning when God created man and made him a **living** soul? What about that fateful day when Adam and Eve ate of the forbidden fruit and realized the consequences of that decision as their heavenly Father described, "for in the day that you eat from it you will surely die" (Genesis 2:17)? What died that day? Physically, they were alive; they were still functioning mentally and emotionally. But they did die...in their spirit.

The New Testament tells us that God created mankind as a triune being…we are comprised of spirit-soul-body. As 1 Thessalonians 5:23 says,

"Now may the God of peace Himself sanctify you entirely; and may your spirit and soul and body be preserved complete, without blame at the coming of our Lord Jesus Christ. Faithful is He who calls you, and He also will bring it to pass."

Essentially, we are spiritual beings with a unique soul of thinking, feeling and choosing that lives in a physical body so we can interact in this earthly environment. Together they form the unique YOU, but the engine or essential nature of the unique you is not your physical appearance or achieved status, nor is it even defined by the inner personality you developed over the years, it is your spirit. So, who are you?

DON'T FREAK OUT, BUT YOU ARE A SPIRIT!

The New Testament tells us that prior to accepting Christ you were separated from Christ and His life...i.e. you were dead in sin. Death does not mean non-existence but rather the absence of, or separation from, life! Just like darkness is simply the absence of light, so death is the absence of Life. You were very much alive physically, mentally and emotionally but were separated from the life of Christ in your spirit.

"Jesus answered, "I am the way and the truth and the life. No one comes to the Father except through me." - John 14:6 NIV

The scripture describes our life before Christ as dead in sin and by nature "children of wrath".

"And you were dead in your trespasses and sins, in which you formerly walked according to the course of this world, according to the prince of the power of the air, of the spirit that is now working in the sons of disobedience. Among them we too all formerly lived in the lusts of our flesh, indulging the desires of the flesh and of the mind, and were by nature children of wrath, even as the rest." -Ephesians 2:1-3

As an "unbeliever", you still had a spirit (or "nature") but were separated from the life of Christ (i.e. dead)! In this state of separation, what or how you think or behave does not affect your very nature. You can try to think positive or become a great humanitarian but your essential nature is still separated from life…that's why the idea of "being good enough" to earn God's favor or pave the way to heaven doesn't make any real sense. The question for the unbeliever then becomes, how do we change who we are? How do we move from death to life?

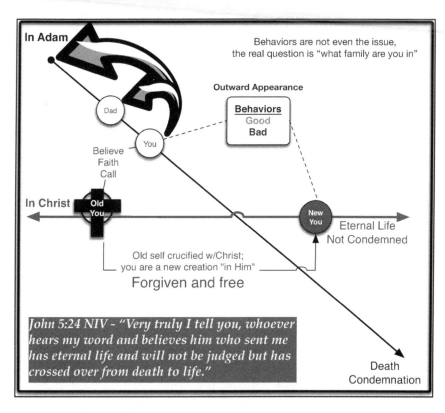

The illustration above "attempts" to answer that question. The diagonal line "In Adam" represents all of us humans born since the beginning of time; Romans 5:12 says,

Therefore, just as through one man sin entered into the world, and death through sin, and so death spread to all men, because all sinned.

22

YOU are on that line! The scripture tells us that we are born through Adam and are, in fact, "in Adam". The idea is not that difficult to grasp. I could say that you are "in" your father or grandfather because if they did not exist, neither would you! So it's not a stretch to say you are in Adam.

In the illustration you will notice that your behavior has no impact on what "line" you are in, it is just your behavior. So the question is, how do we move from "in Adam" to "in Christ", or how do change our location and switch families? If not by good works, then how?

When a person understands and believes that Jesus Christ is who He said He is, the Lord of all, their only hope for salvation and a relationship with their heavenly Father, God makes the exchange from death to life. Specifically, a person believes that God came to this earth (Jesus) for the purpose of rescuing each one of us from death by offering Himself as our substitute for the penalty of sin. Perhaps you get hung up on the word "believe"? Well, the scripture provides other words that may register with you better (receive, believe, faith, call, et. al.), but no matter what the word, it is ALWAYS by His grace.

When you accept Christ as YOUR Savior (believe, faith, call), an incredible transaction takes place in the blink of an eye. The old you "in Adam" is "crucified with Christ" and the new you is resurrected "in Christ"; God exchanges your old sin nature (or old self) for a new righteous nature and joins Himself with your new spirit, moving you from "in Adam" to "in Christ" (or from death to life - you are now joined to the Way, the Truth and the Life).

You are now brand, spanking new. You are no longer IN ADAM but are now IN CHRIST. According to 2 Corinthians 5:17

"therefore if anyone is in Christ, he is a new creature; the old things passed away; behold, new things have come."

That's why Galatians 6:15 tells us with respect to any behavior or ritual,

"for neither is circumcision anything, nor uncircumcision, but a new creation."

You may look the same, but a dramatic transformation has taken place inside. You are now a new creation, forgiven, holy and righteous in Him.
Paul tells us in Romans 6:6-7

"knowing this, that our old self was crucified with Him, in order that our body of sin might be done away with, so that we would no longer be slaves to sin; for he who has died is freed from sin."

Folks, the old you is dead; it's time to recognize that truth and the fact that you are a brand new creation in Christ! It's a done deal! With the old self gone, the "body of sin" is "done away with" or a better translation, "that the body ruled by sin might be done away with" or rendered powerless and unproductive.

THE OLD YOU *DIED*; YOU ARE BRAND *NEW* IN CHRIST!

As you unpack this idea of identity, you begin to see scripture with a whole different perspective. Those verses you once thought earned you righteousness through obedience now point to the righteousness you already have in Christ! What changed? Nothing, well, everything! As a believer in Christ your new identity was established the moment you believed...you just didn't know it!
It's interesting how one piece of information changes things...you don't behave to get more righteous, you

understand and believe your new righteous identity and your behavior begins to take care of itself. The world, however, is quite different. We're brought up in a cause and effect world system. If you do this you will get that which is the very opposite idea of God's grace. Sometimes it's challenging to believe and accept the grace that is ours in Christ!

We often interpret scripture in light of our own experience; "certainly this verse does not mean that I am righteous, did you see what I did the other night?" We see our true identity in the physical realm not the spiritual realm and believe our behavior defines who we are, but that's just not true. We are a spiritual being living in a physical body NOT a physical being with spiritual qualities...it makes a HUGE difference!

This body will eventually get old and die; it is a necessary and important part of your time here on earth BUT your body and your behavior do not define you...you are a spiritual being that has been made brand new in Christ and united with Him for eternity. Your works may define your reputation and your sin may (and does) have consequences on this earth, but Christ defined your identity when He conquered sin and death on the cross and made you the righteous, holy, pure, complete and lovely person you are in Him...that is the core of your being, the real you that is in complete union with the Savior of the world, ready to express that victorious Life through your human experience. His desire is to use the entire you, spirit, soul and body to share His love and grace to a needy world.

Life transformation

The foundation of experiencing victory is understanding our identity in Christ. Consistent victory will be your experience as God transforms your thinking over time to align with the truth. But how does that transformation work? Let's take a look...literally! What do I mean? Well in a mirror of course!

So, how do you see you? When you look in a mirror, what or who is looking back at you? Do you see a failure? A no good sinner? One who just can't cut it? Or, do you see what God sees...a brand new creation radiating the glory of the Lord?

"But to this day whenever Moses is read, a veil lies over their heart; but whenever a person turns to the Lord, the veil is taken away. Now the Lord is the Spirit, and where the Spirit of the Lord is, there is liberty. But we all, with unveiled face, beholding as in a mirror the glory of the Lord, are being transformed into the same image from glory to glory, just as from the Lord, the Spirit."
-2 Corinthians 3:15–18

WHAT DO YOU SEE IN THE MIRROR?

Do you see it? We had a veil over our heart and our understanding, but when we turned to the Lord, receiving His forgiveness and grace through the cross, that veil was taken away and we can now begin to see reality. God is in the business of transforming our life here on this planet to align with the reality of the new creation He has already formed through the cross. His desire is for you and I to see, understand and believe the truth.

Unfortunately, many can not see past their own failures. Newsflash! Your failure and defeat have been taken care of at the cross; you are now an overcomer in Christ! Stop looking at your past or even your present mess or rotten circumstances. Don't focus on the "what ifs" and the "I wish" or the "I'll never"...choose to believe, apart from all reason if you must, that God knows what He is doing and loves you right now! Focus on the truth that God HAS made you a brand new creation through Christ. Understand and believe that you are holy and righteous because of Christ and every need you have is satisfied through Him. I am not talking about the power of positive thinking, I am talking about the power of TRUTH thinking.

WE'RE NOT TALKING ABOUT THE POWER OF POSITIVE THINKING, BUT THE POWER OF TRUTH THINKING

Perhaps you are saying, "well, that will be true once we're in heaven, but right here, right now is a different story." Really? Think about it. Although I agree we will have a new, glorified body in heaven, the real you has been changed in the here and now! "Oh no", you might say, "that's just how God sees me cause the real me is a mess!" Wait a second... are you saying that you see yourself more clearly than God sees you? Do you somehow think God is fooling Himself and looking at you through rose-colored glasses or some other such non-sense? No, no, no...in heaven you will finally see the REAL you which you are missing right now because you are believing a lie (or at best misinformed). Don't miss it! The REAL YOU is NOT a mess, it has been radically changed, transformed and united with Christ and therein lies the "battle". Your experience may be messy at times but the reality is, you have been radically changed.

So, what do you see when you look in the mirror? As

you begin see what God sees, to believe and accept the truth about the new YOU and see it in the mirror, God will handle the outward transformation "from glory to glory" (2 Corinthians 3:18). God sees the REAL you, the righteous and holy you, the problem is you and I often see something different. Remember, what God says IS truth and what God sees IS reality. Give yourself a break and don't focus on where you are spiritually or behaviorally, rest in the fact that you are God's loved, righteous, forgiven, accepted and valued child, secure in His care.

Don't worry, you're not the only one blinded by your failure and defeat, and living in this world doesn't help at times either! So before you begin to process how to deal with temptation, you MUST be grounded in this foundational, life changing, perspective-bending reality of your new identity in Christ...but how? Well, it's all over the new testament in various ideas, but for now, let's just call it "renewing your mind". What you will soon realize is that the real battle is fought in your mind.

Paul begs us in the letter to Romans 12:1-2,

"therefore I urge you, brethren, by the mercies of God, to present your bodies a living and holy sacrifice, acceptable to God, which is your spiritual service of worship. And do not be conformed to this world, but be transformed by the renewing of your mind, so that you may prove what the will of God is, that which is good and acceptable and perfect."

Go ahead, present that body of yours to God as a living and holy sacrifice. You might be thinking, "Wait, God may not want this body quite yet"! Don't be silly, you are already loved and accepted body, soul and spirit; His desire is to express His very life through you right now (that's the best kind of worship by the way)! I get it though, you may be concerned about your consistency or other behavior issues.

Let God worry about your consistency, He wants to love, live, encourage and so much more through you, so present that body of yours to God. How? By faith! Step out by faith in humility, kindness, love, victory and power...the new you created in Christ! No need to wait until you get your act together, God is transforming your act right now. Renew your thinking. Start walking by faith and believing the truth.

LET GOD WORRY ABOUT YOUR CONSISTENCY!

The word "renewing" in Romans 12:2 is the greek word *anakainosis* and carries the idea of a renovation. As with any renovation, it starts with a demo or demolition day. You tear down those old lies and believe the truth that God reveals, and the renovation of your belief system begins. As the renovation continues, the outward transformation or *metamorphoo* begins to take shape. The unique person that you are, wrapped up in the holiness and righteousness of Christ, begins to express itself through your body, words, behavior, attitude and more. Neediness is replaced with a quiet confidence; inevitable failure is replaced with consistent, overcoming victory; striving and struggling is replaced with grace and rest. Your believing and faith do not cause the transformation; you don't faith something into existence. Your believing and faith in God's truth unleash the real you "in Christ" locked up by the lies you were believing and allows the power of God to flow freely through your life. As we often say on our Freedom From Addiction webinars, lies will keep you in spiritual bondage and defeat but the truth will set you free (John 8:32).

This is just a start. Renew your mind with the truth BEFORE the temptation comes raging at your door and trust me, it will come. How, where, and when it will come is different for each person. So, are you ready?

Questions

Define life and death? How could someone be the "walking dead"?

What happens to your old spirit, or sin nature, or the old you when you receive Christ?

How do we experience transformation in our every day life?

Why is it so hard to believe the truth of our identity in Christ?

How can YOU present your body to God this week?

3

Are You Ready?

Trials and temptations

James 1:2-12

"Consider it all joy, my brethren, when you encounter various trials, knowing that the testing of your faith produces endurance. And let endurance have its perfect result, so that you may be perfect and complete, lacking in nothing.

But if any of you lacks wisdom, let him ask of God, who gives to all generously and without reproach, and it will be given to him. But he must ask in faith without any doubting, for the one who doubts is like the surf of the sea, driven and tossed by the wind. For that man ought not to expect that he will receive anything from the Lord, being a double-minded man, unstable in all his ways.

But the brother of humble circumstances is to glory in his high position; and the rich man is to glory in his humiliation, because like flowering grass he will pass away. For the sun rises with a scorching wind and withers the grass; and its flower falls off and the beauty of its appearance is destroyed; so too the rich man in the midst of his pursuits will fade away.

Blessed is a man who perseveres under trial; for once he has been approved, he will receive the crown of life which the Lord has promised to those who love Him."

Trials and temptation are common place, but did you know in the New Testament the same word is used for these two distinctly different ideas? It is imperative we read the context carefully to understand what the author is intending.

Back in the day, the New Testament audience most likely understood the different meanings as a matter of course. We do the same thing using the same word which could mean something different in a particular context. For example, we pray FOR rain (we are asking God to provide us rain); we also spray FOR bugs. We don't spray in order to get more bugs but rather because we have bugs and want to keep them away. How about the word SEASON…a SEASON of life is different than a SEASON of the year which is different than when we SEASON our food (English as second language must be so challenging). Same word used differently, just depends on the context.

"*Peirasmos*" can mean a trial, test, calamity OR can mean a temptation to evil…same word, different meaning. For purposes of this book we will use the term "Trial" for challenging circumstances in our life and "Temptation" for the enticement to do evil or sin. The vast majority of our time in this book will focus on the idea of temptation but for just a moment, let's talk about TRIALS since James introduces this idea before going into the process of temptation.

Trials TEST our FAITH; Temptation DECEIVES our THINKING

As James 1:2 tells us, trials are for the "testing of [our] faith" and we should "consider it all joy" when trials come our way. Now think about it…do you REALLY think we should be jumping for joy when we are tempted to do evil? Of course not! Life happens. Illness, financial difficulties, relational troubles, job issues and more. As we trust God in the midst of these trials we develop a type of "endurance" or "perseverance" that only comes in those difficult circumstances (kinda like exercise, your body goes through a challenge but comes out better over time). We often need wisdom in the midst of trials to figure out our next steps, and we are encouraged to ask for it! And whether rich or poor, we humbly trust that God is working all things for our good, even as the storm rages all around us. At the end of the day, and I mean the literal end of our lives once we have passed this mortal test, we receive the crown of life as God promised for those who love Him (and that's all believers, by the way, for nothing can separate you from His love).

So why did James toss these two ideas of trials and

temptation together in his letter? If you think about it, Christians in his day were going through all kinds of trials, hardships, persecutions and more. James knew that when navigating these trials, temptation will often slither our way enticing us to evil (perhaps tempting us to short-cut the trial through lying, cheating, stealing, or something more devious, or even escaping the trial for a momentary "high" just to get through it). So what is the bottom line? Trials test our faith; temptation deceives our thinking. Trials are endured; temptation is overcome.

TRIALS ARE ENDURED; TEMPTATION IS OVERCOME.

I know many who read 1 Corinthians 10:13 as encouragement for their temptation (and that's fine), but I see it as encouragement in our trials (remember, same greek word).

"No temptation has overtaken you but such as is common to man; and God is faithful, who will not allow you to be tempted beyond what you are able, but with the temptation will provide the way of escape also, so that you will be able to endure it."
- 1 Corinthians 10:13.

The encouragement here is that God is faithful in the midst of our trials; He is in control, He will not allow a trial that is more than we can bear through the vast resources in Christ and will provide the way of escape. Wait, escape from what? It could be an escape from the trial OR the provision of an oasis in the midst of the trial. Either way, God will provide an escape so we can endure the trial (please note, we generally do not endure temptation, we are told to RUN).

I do believe God can and will use trials to break our dependency on our old ways (the "flesh" or false sense of self, etc)...that is often one of the temptations. In the midst of the trial, just like the children of Israel, we are tempted to lose faith and turn away from our loving heavenly Father to follow our old way of thinking and behaving.

"Now you followed my teaching, conduct, purpose, faith, patience, love, perseverance, persecutions, and sufferings, such as happened to me at Antioch, at Iconium and at Lystra; what persecutions I endured, and out of them all the Lord rescued me!" -2 Tim. 3:10–11.

Generally speaking, you can have a temptation without a trial, but every trial includes one or more temptations.

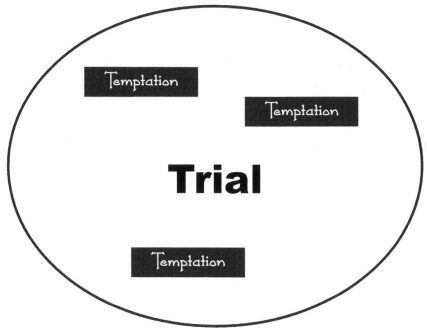

So, where does God fit in to this scenario...is God tempting me to sin? Let's take a look.

Don't blame God

Now, before we focus on the process of temptation in James 1:14-15, notice the very strong statement just prior in verse 13: "Let no one say when he is tempted, "I am being tempted by God"; for God cannot be tempted by evil, and He Himself does not tempt anyone". When you and I are tempted to do or think evil, it is not a test from God to see how much we can endure. As we said earlier, God will test and build our faith but will not tempt us to do evil. God is not in the business of encouraging our failure but has provided us the means to rise above all this stuff through His victorious life. So do not get confused here and think God is "tempting" you.

God Is NOT Tempting You!

And here is the cool thing…Jesus understands where you are in the struggle. He's been there. He's not saying, "Oh, there they go again", "why don't they get their act together" or "what a loser." No way. He sympathizes…He agonizes… He loves no matter what.

"For we do not have a high priest who cannot sympathize with our weaknesses, but One who has been tempted in all things as we are, yet without sin." -Hebrews 4:15

But wait! Didn't we just read that "God can not be tempted by evil"? Absolutely yes. So, if Jesus is God, how could He be tempted? Remember, Jesus was 100% man AND 100% God…He did not allow His divinity to supersede His humanity. Jesus operated in the power of the Spirit…and so can you.

While we're on earth temptation is not going anywhere, it's something we will have to deal with on a regular basis. The question is, how are you dealing with it? Are you trying to battle temptation in your own strength? Are you fighting these battles through your best human strategies? Have you given up any hope for a consistent, victorious, overcoming experience? Don't worry, we've all been there...you're not alone. God has provided everything we need to live the victorious Christian life, but the question remains "why are we failing on what seems like a regular basis"?

BLAMING IS NEVER THE ANSWER

Now, you may think "if only I was brought up in a different family" or "if my circumstances were different" temptation would not be such an issue? Let's ponder that for a moment. For those who believe the literal story of Adam and Eve (which I do), they lived in a perfect environment and had never experienced sin YET were tempted and blew it just the same. What's up with that? Now I'm not in any way trying to diminish the difficulty of your circumstances; I've spoken with many folks over the years and heard countless stories of extremely difficult and abusive environments, but living in a perfect, sinless environment with all your needs provided for, walking and talking directly with God and still blowing it? Perhaps environment is not the primary issue when it comes to temptation (although it can certainly be a contributing factor). I think we need to dive in a little deeper in this idea of temptation.

When things go bad we tend to blame, don't we? It's almost a knee jerk reaction for many. "Well, if God didn't create that snake we wouldn't be in this mess?" Really? I guess we could also say if God never created you and I we wouldn't be tempted nor even having this conversation, right? Yet He chose to create us, knowing we would be tempted, knowing we would fail at times AND chose to pay the penalty of ALL our sin on the cross so we could enjoy His presence forever. Instead of blaming God for our mess why not thank God for the cross, for His forgiveness, grace and power to overcome all this temptation (I know, we're getting to that part soon). Knowing how we would all screw up, God decided you and I were worth it.

OWN YOUR CHOICES AND ACCEPT HIS GRACE

While we are at it, be careful blaming others for the choices you make or are making right now. Blaming can be a sign that you have been hurt, you are angry and you have yet to forgive the other person. Like those in Corinth struggling to forgive a particular individual, choose to forgive the one who has hurt you,

"so that no advantage would be taken of [you] by Satan, for we are not ignorant of his schemes." -2 Corinthians 2:11

Blaming can also be a point of pride where we do not want to look weak. We simply can not own our poor decisions. We compare ourselves to others and/or hold ourselves to some impossible standard; we fail to see that this too is yet another enemy strategy to keep us from experiencing Christ. Let go of your reputation. Let go of your pride. Let go of your false belief that you must always act perfect. Choose humility. Choose the cross. Choose grace.

"We do not dare to classify or compare ourselves with some who commend themselves. When they measure themselves by themselves and compare themselves with themselves, they are not wise." -2 Corinthians 10:12

"Humble yourselves in the presence of the Lord, and He will exalt you." -James 4:10

"Have this attitude in yourselves which was also in Christ Jesus, who, although He existed in the form of God, did not regard equality with God a thing to be grasped, but emptied Himself, taking the form of a bond-servant, and being made in the likeness of men. Being found in appearance as a man, He humbled Himself by becoming obedient to the point of death, even death on a cross." -Philippians 2:5–8

Temptation is a part of life on this planet. James 1:14-15 describes the struggle we all face on a daily basis; the "Battle Blueprint" is simply a diagram to illustrate the reality of the struggle and a strategy to experience victory (don't worry, it is NOT a list of dos and don'ts...we've been there and done that, right?). I hope, in the next few pages, to help you dissect this "Battle Blueprint" and understand in more depth the "truth that will set you free" where victory becomes your natural course of life.

Questions

What's the difference between "trials" and "temptation"?

Does God tempt you? Why or why not?

What is the one thing many do (as Adam and Eve both did) when things go wrong? How might that be dangerous?

Are you in the midst of any trials at the moment? Describe them. List, if appropriate, any temptations you encountered in the midst of those trials?

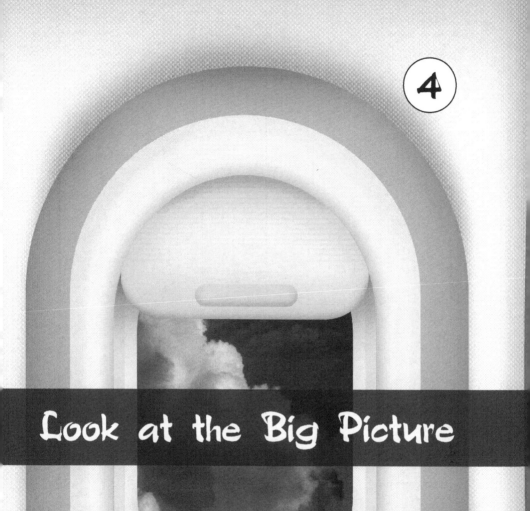

Look at the Big Picture

BATTLE BLUEPRINT
JAMES 1:14-15

carried away - *(Exelko) to draw out; lure forth: in hunting and fishing as game is lured from its hiding place*
lust - *(Epithumia) desire, craving, longing, desire for what is forbidden, lust*
entice - *(Deleazo) - to bait; catch by a bait; to beguile or deceive*

Each One

carried away

by his own lust

Enticed

Tempters: Satan, World →

Our "own lust" or "flesh" is developed over time as patterns of thinking and behaving; temptation is where we are baited and deceived to fulfill our needs, drives, passions and/or desires after the flesh (apart from Christ) .

Tempted

Experience Victory

Experience Forgiveness

Experiencing victory is believing the truth that we are dead to sin and alive to God, trusting the sufficiency of Christ's life within to overcome temptation.
1 Cor. 15:57, 1 John 4:4, 5:4

Steps to experience Christ's victory

1. Expose the lie
2. Embrace the truth
3. Act by faith

Gal. 5:16

(Sullambano) - to seize for one's self

Sin is where we seize the bait to fulfill our own needs, drives, passion and/or desires thus missing the mark of God's power and grace

Conceived

Sin

Philippians 4:6-7

Give thanks that ALL our sins are forgiven at the cross, even this one!
"...having forgiven us all our transgressions"
- Colossians 2:13

Accomplished

Ineffective faith
James 2:14-26; 1 Cor. 9:27

Blind and forgetful faith
2 Peter 1:9

Spiritual bondage
Romans 6:12-19; Galatians 4:8-10

Death

FreeNHim
living the truth

The Battle Blueprint

Over the next several chapters we will dissect The Battle Blueprint diagram, but for now let's begin with an overview. The diagram is my attempt to draw a picture of what I see when reading James 1:14-15. I then take what I know of God's grace and victory to offer a visual perspective of the temptation process. In the next few pages we will take some time to focus on each section of the diagram, but at this stage I'd like to run through the diagram as a whole. Yes, I may repeat myself just a little bit in the later pages but that's how we learn!

The circles in the middle of the Battle Blueprint are key words in the passage. "Each one" of us is "tempted" and at some point that temptation can birth "sin"; when finished, that sin (and all sin) results in "death". Can you relate? I think it is somewhat self-evident. We've all been tempted, made a bad decision and the result was not what was promised by the temptation. It always ends bad, perhaps not immediately, but eventually "death" comes knocking at our door (and no, I do not necessarily mean physical death, but more on that point later).

There is a process of "drawing us away" that culminates in a point of temptation. The process could be so fast we can barely identify what happened, or the process might be like drops of water against a stone that slowly degrades the integrity of the surface. No matter HOW you are tempted, the point is you WILL be tempted. It is a fact of life, a fact of our human existence on this planet. Yes, there are some temptations that you can avoid (and I encourage you to do so) BUT get real, you will NEVER escape temptation. How's that for some encouragement! Seriously, it's not all doom and gloom, in fact, far from it!

Do you really think your heavenly Father has left you on your own to face all these challenges? Are you believing the lie that "if it is to be, it's up to me!" What utter nonsense for the believer in Christ. I do NOT want to minimize the sometimes agonizing issues, temptations, challenges that we may face, I just want to maximize the power of our omnipotent God who lives within us. I want to maximize the incredible grace and forgiveness of our heavenly Father, and even better, the victory we have through Him.

DON'T MINIMIZE TEMPTATION AND SIN, JUST MAXIMIZE GOD'S POWER AND GRACE

In James 1:14-15, James describes the natural progression of sin and death that begins when we lose focus and are tempted, continues when the temptation takes hold and results in a bad choice to sin, and ends with the result of sin, which is death. James was continuing his initial thought from the beginning of the chapter about trials and answering the question if God might be tempting them in the midst of those trials to do evil. Basically, James might say, "let's start at the beginning guys...even in the midst of your trials, you are responsible for your choices and God is not the one tempting you to do evil...you are drawn away and enticed by your own lusts". That's why James ended the discussion with,

Do not be deceived, my beloved brethren. 17 Every good thing given and every perfect gift is from above, coming down from the Father of lights, with whom there is no variation or shifting shadow. 18 In the exercise of His will He brought us forth by the word of truth, so that we would be a kind of first fruits among His creatures. - James 1:16-18

James point in what I call the "Battle Blueprint" was not outlining how we experience victory, but revealing the natural progression of one who is "deceived", **so "do not be deceived"**.

Remember what his brother Jesus said in John 8:32, 36

and you will know the truth, and the truth will make you free. So if the Son makes you free, you will be free indeed.

My desire in the Battle Blueprint is to show you that temptation does not equal sin, and that in Christ we have a path to experience victory. How? Because we already have victory through the cross and resurrection of Jesus Christ. The trick, if you will, is learning how to experience what is already ours in Christ.

The normal Christian life is one that includes temptation but follows the path to experience victory and life. The unfortunate reality is that many are in what they feel is an unbreakable sin-forgiveness loop of defeat and despair. Let me be very clear...there is a way out of what seems like your hopeless situation. There is HOPE.

I want you to take a break from all your self-analysis...we all do it, but for now just suspend it for a moment. I want you to take a small step of faith with me. I want you to read the verse I am about to share with you and CHOOSE to believe it is true for YOU...not just true for the others in your group, or those you admire, but true for YOU.

seeing that His divine power has granted to us everything pertaining to life and godliness, through the true knowledge of Him who called us by His own glory and excellence. -2 Peter 1:3

Did you catch that? You have everything you need right now for life and godliness. There is nothing else required for you to experience life and godliness. Church is awesome; groups are fantastic; reading the Bible is incredible. Life and godliness, however, are only found "in Christ", and that is where you are. You are "in Him" and He is in you. You are a brand new creation infused with the very Life of Christ in the person of the Holy Spirit. You ARE victorious and you are free.

I want you to continue reading and absorbing the "truth that will set you free". If you have not downloaded it yet, you can get a full copy of the Battle Blueprint diagram at *https://www.StopFightingStartLiving.com.* I have tweaked this diagram over the years and am very intentional with my words, especially "experiencing victory" and "experiencing forgiveness".

As we continue together, I want you to STOP praying for victory and STOP begging God to forgive you (you already have victory and you are already forgiven, even if you are not yet experiencing that victory or feeling very forgiven). Take a breath. You are no more righteous and holy with every victory nor are you less righteous or less spiritual with every defeat.

The battle before the battle

Look, we're all faced with temptation...that's right, every single one of us. One thing you must remember, temptation is NOT sin (as you can clearly see in the scripture and illustrated by the diagram). Temptation by definition can result in sin but is clearly a separate issue. Jesus was *"tempted in all things as we are, yet without sin"* -Hebrews 4:15. There is no need to feel guilty or ashamed when you're tempted...it shows you're absolutely normal!

Jesus Christ was "tempted in **all things**" (my emphasis) and yet He did not sin; that fact alone should give us resounding hope. As we mentioned earlier, Jesus did not live His life according to the divine privilege afforded Him as Son of God, but rather submitted to the Father in the power of the Holy Spirit as a human being and experienced victory over temptation. Guess what? We can do the same.

The "first Adam" blew it; the "last Adam" (Jesus) was victorious. Remember, when you accepted Christ as Savior, an incredible transaction took place. To "bottom line it" for the moment, the old you died and the new you was created and placed "in Christ", AND, the omnipotent Son of God in the person of the Holy Spirit came to live on the inside of your body where you are joined with Him, in union with Christ in your spirit!

There are some incredible verses in the Bible that describe the mystery of God coming to dwell inside of you and me... check them out!

"that is the Spirit of truth, whom the world cannot receive, because it does not see Him or know Him, but you know Him because He abides with you and will be in you." -John 14:17

"but these have been written so that you may believe that Jesus is the Christ, the Son of God; and that believing you may have life in His name."-John 20:31. [Of course, Jesus IS Life – John 14:6!]

"to whom God willed to make known what is the riches of the glory of this mystery among the Gentiles, which is Christ in you, the hope of glory." -Colossians 1:27

"For all of you who were baptized into Christ have clothed yourselves with Christ." -Galatians 3:27

"But by His doing you are in Christ Jesus, who became to us wisdom from God, and righteousness and sanctification, and redemption." -1 Corinthians 1:30

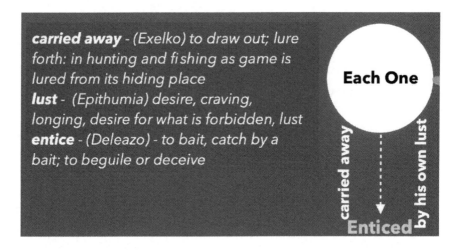

carried away - *(Exelko)* to draw out; lure forth: in hunting and fishing as game is lured from its hiding place
lust - *(Epithumia)* desire, craving, longing, desire for what is forbidden, lust
entice - *(Deleazo)* - to bait, catch by a bait; to beguile or deceive

Each One

carried away

by his own lust

Enticed

The Battle Blueprint diagram with the circle "each one" at the top is where we begin the process. It's here where you can be proactive. How? Understand your true position in the temptation struggle before the struggle even begins. Christ has already won the war and you are in Him! You've already won! So what's the problem? Our experience does not always align with that truth! Most often it simply doesn't "feel" like we've won, does it? You may not realize this but your feelings tend to follow your thinking, so it's time to rethink your position. You're not fighting to win the war, that's already accomplished. It really is a done deal. It's time for you to inherit the land and walk in the victory won at the cross. That's right, you are already victorious in Christ because He won the victory!

I do not want to minimize temptation, it often feels like a battle and in a sense, it really is one, a battle of the mind. Are you facing temptation as a battle to be fought and won (or lost), or are you facing temptation as triumphant conqueror in a war that has already been won by the Lord Jesus Christ Himself. If the former, we often end up devising a "self-defense" strategy; if the latter, we walk in the victory already won.

TEMPTATION IS NOT A BATTLE TO BE WON, IT'S AN OPPORTUNITY TO EXPERIENCE HIS VICTORY

"Self-defense" programs are abundant in the world…when it comes to living life, the self-defense options include the power of positive thinking, defining rules to keep yourself from sinning, strengthening your weakness, I think I can…I think I can, etc. If you're depending on strategies like these to experience victory (or some hybrid with God's "help") you're in for a major disappointment. The ultimate "battle" is not about good or bad behavior, the battle is all about faith…who are you, who are you trusting in, relying on, depending on as your very life, strength and source.

Self-defense simply does not work in the spiritual realm because it assumes you still need to fix and defend your "self" which has already been "fixed" at the cross. The scripture advocates a different approach: "the truth will set you free", "boast about my weakness, so that the power of

49

Christ may dwell in me", "I can do all things through Him who strengthens me", etc. If the basis of your strategy in the struggle of temptation is anything other than the resting in the victorious Christ in you, your strategy is seriously flawed. At this "each one" stage, make time to dwell on the truths of scripture and affirm who you are and your position in Christ *"Who is your Life"* (Colossians 3:4) BEFORE the battle comes your way (and trust me, the temptation will come and come and come again). No matter how many times it comes, the truth is you're already victorious "in Him".

THERE IS NOTHING MORE FOR YOU TO DO UNLESS YOU BELIEVE YOU CAN ADD MORE TO WHAT CHRIST HAS ALREADY DONE; NEWSFLASH, "IT IS FINISHED".

One question always comes up at this point so let's address it right now..."so tell me, what can or must I do?" The real answer to that question is absolutely nothing! Christ has already done it all; my job and your job is to simply believe and enter into the victory He has provided. I know, that can be somewhat difficult to grasp.

To be fair, **there are many things you can "do" to help you understand the truth that there is really nothing more for you to do**...ok, that sounded a bit weird and/or contradictory, just go with it for now. "Doing" is all over the New Testament BUT with the understanding that, as a believer, you are already made new "in Christ". Don't knock the doing, just don't depend on the doing to add more to what Christ has already done!

The next page has a few ideas for you to consider; doing them will not add to the victory that is already yours in Christ but may encourage your faith just a bit.

"So faith comes from hearing, and hearing by the word of Christ."
-Romans 10:17

Ideas before the battle at the "Each One" stage

- Meditate / Memorize scripture, especially around your identity in Christ. Personalize the verses, where appropriate, and say them out loud (I would do this privately, you don't want to make a scene).
- Take time and listen to uplifting worship music around the truth...music will reach to the deepest parts of your soul. Remember when David played for King Saul to drive away the evil? Music is powerful.
- Take a few minutes each day or every other day and spend time with the Lord reading His Word, praying, learning, listening but remember, this will NOT gain you any more power of victory than you already have in Christ. It will, however, remind you, comfort you, encourage and strengthen you in the faith.

Of course, the above ideas are often confused with something you must DO to GAIN victory...do NOT fall into that trap (I know many who do all kinds of spiritual exercises like the above only to fail miserably)! The activities I describe are all derived from scripture and can point you to the cross and the victory you already have in Christ but sadly are sometimes used as another strategy of self-defense! Before, during and after the battle rages, fortify your soul with the truth that sets you free.

Let's take a look at the actual process of temptation outlined in this "Battle Blueprint" in more detail.

Questions

What insights can you draw from looking at the Battle Blueprint diagram?

What does it mean to "experience victory" and "experience forgiveness"?

What is the battle before the battle? How can you be proactive at this stage?

Describe the trap that many well-intentioned Christians fail to see when dealing with this issue of temptation? Can you describe ways in the past you fell victim to this trap?

5

And It Begins...

Carried away

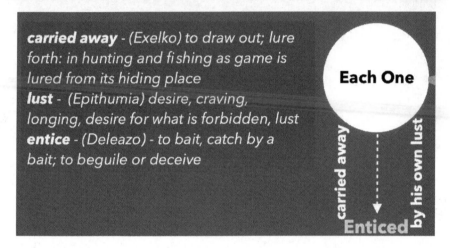

carried away - (Exelko) to draw out; lure forth: in hunting and fishing as game is lured from its hiding place

lust - (Epithumia) desire, craving, longing, desire for what is forbidden, lust

entice - (Deleazo) - to bait, catch by a bait; to beguile or deceive

Each One

carried away

Enticed

by his own lust

OK...here we go. We've all been there; no one is exempt. You are tempted. Your temptation may be in the context of relationships with that special someone. Thoughts are racing in your head, "that's not fair", "he always gets his way", "she's thinks she's better", "why do I always have to...", "he does not appreciate me", "if she loved me she would" and the list goes on.

Your temptation may be public for anyone to see or private and personal, hidden in the fortress of your mind with thoughts that attack your very foundation as a man or woman, that pierce the most sacred place of who you are, why you exist, your purpose, peace, value, and life. The temptation could be anywhere in between. Regardless of the type of temptation, we know that "each one" of us is tempted. You are NOT the only one!

Temptation is a normal part of the Christian experience. Notice, I did not say yielding to temptation is normal. We often "fail" because we don't understand the process and how to experience victory, but temptation itself is just a part of life. If you believe you are somehow different, that your problems are way above the norm and this Christian victory stuff just doesn't apply, then the battle is over before it begins. I do not mean to trivialize your circumstances, traumas or other life events...some of which, I'm sure, simply defy our human understanding and impact the intensity of your temptation struggle, but you must not give in to the lie that "this doesn't apply, I am just too different".

Temptation Is Rooted In Deception

Jesus can certainly identify here. The cross was the worst injustice ever done on a human level. The torture, shame, humiliation and painful death on a roman cross should have been unbearable and the temptations that accompanied that must have been enormous. How often have we been tempted to lash out for simply being misunderstood? Or after being hurt, tempted to either hurt others or ourselves in response? Yeah, I think it would be a good idea to keep reading, give it a chance, knowing Jesus has been through more than we can imagine yet come through it in resurrection splendor (and remember, Jesus' half brother is writing this letter! Can you imagine if YOUR half-brother was God in the flesh growing up? Blaming Jesus probably did not work in James' home; I bet you would have had temptations galore!).

In James 1:14 the temptation process is so clearly detailed. Let's take a look. "But each one is tempted when he is..."

Carried away and enticed

The Greek word for "carried away" is *exelko* meaning to draw out (or even drag out) or lure, as in hunting or fishing. "Enticed" is the Greek word *deleazo* meaning to catch by bait or to deceive or beguile. Very simply, we are deceived or baited to sin against God.

Can you relate here? Do you recognize times where you were lured into complacency or drawn away from your quiet, confidence in Christ? Perhaps you remember a time where your mind wandered a bit and eventually got lost with anxious or fearful thoughts, fantasies or sexual scenarios, past hurts and regrets or worse? The "carried away" may start slowly, even over hours or days, but at some point we may feel like we are being dragged against our will with this lure hooked in our mouth. We feel trapped, like we can't get away. Something or someone is fishing for our soul to feast on our failure, to bask in the glory of catching another big one and pose for a picture; they are reeling us in and we feel like our only option is to give in so we can hopefully get some relief!

LUST IS A DESIRE TO SATISFY LEGITIMATE NEEDS, DRIVES OR PASSIONS OUTSIDE OF GOD'S DESIGN

Who is casting the line and yanking our chain? We see in scripture that specific, targeted forces are deceiving and setting traps to derail our relationships, faith, character, ministry...our very life. Who are they? We'll get to that soon enough, but what are these forces (or tempters as I call them in the diagram) using to deceive and lure us to sin? Can you believe it, they are using our "own lust" against us. Notice, it is our OWN lust.

By his own lust

Lust is the Greek word *epithumia*, which is a desire or craving, especially for something forbidden. The driving force behind lust, in my opinion, is a legitimate, God-given need, drive or passion. When you think of lust, what is the first idea that comes to mind? You guessed it, sex. Sex is one of many legitimate needs that can become lust when we seek it's fulfillment outside of God's design; security, acceptance, significance, intimacy, peace, fulfillment, belonging, etc. are also needs that demand fulfillment. Your drive and/or passion could be a ministry, cause, niche, mission, life purpose, etc. that commands your attention.

Lust is simply a desire to satisfy legitimate needs, drives or passions outside of God's design. Often we think this is characterized solely by negative behavior…not necessarily. Temptation is extremely versatile and is customized and personalized for each of us (our OWN lust); the sin we're tempted with could be outward behaviors as well as inward thoughts, attitudes, motivation, etc. It's possible the temptation before you, in all human understanding, appears as a positive and worthwhile act, even ministry oriented, but the internal motivation/attitude is the real issue. Remember, in Jesus' day religion and some religious leaders looked good on the outside *"but inside they are full of dead men's bones"* -Matthew 23:27…their temptation was how to perform for others and/or manipulate for personal gain, approval or control.

Temptation, when we break it down, is where you are baited and seemingly dragged away and deceived to fulfill your God-given needs, drive, passion and/or desires (negative or positive) apart from Christ and His design.

Most often the deception occurs first in our thinking, ignites our emotions and culminates in a sinful action (i.e. a behavior or performance apart from Christ). Over the course of our lives, we developed many ways to meet and fulfill those needs in our own strength and resources…the scripture calls that "flesh", basically, living like the "old" or "former self".

Flesh - your former self

What is "flesh" and how is that word used in scripture? Well, "flesh" is a broad term and must be defined in the context of a given passage. The biblical word for flesh is *"sarx"* and can mean a number of things depending on the context. The scripture describes FLESH as our human body, human efforts and/or desires in this earthly body (Romans 7:14, 18, 8:3); it is defined as our lineage and heritage (Romans 1:3, Philippians 3:3-5), our own self-efforts (Philippians 3:6), our bad behaviors (Galatians 5:19), our efforts to be good (Galatians 3:3) and even our former sin nature with its manifested behaviors (Galatians 5:24). It can be further described as "the law of sin which is in my members" (Romans 7:23). The point I'm making is ALWAYS keep EVERYTHING in context.

Don't misunderstand, the physical body (physical flesh) in and of itself is not sinful or evil, it simply carries a "flesh" cancer that courses through its veins as a result of the curse. Before accepting Christ as our Savior, my actual "self" or "nature" or "spirit" was sin and in the broad use of the word, also "flesh". As a new creation in Christ, that old self has been crucified with Christ, dead and gone, and we now have a brand new nature. The physical body, however, does not receive a complete makeover until our own physical death and resurrection. Have you noticed that your body tends to wear down a bit as you get older? That's validation of the curse and a wonderful picture of the result of sin (it just wears you down).

Over time each one of us developed and customized our own "flesh", our own unique ways to make life work apart from God's grace (get our way, defend ourselves, meet our needs, etc.)…it began in our childhood and we've honed those skills ever since. For some, tantrums always resulted in getting our way; for others, sulking and pouting worked wonders and for still others, winsome negotiation seemed to do the trick. We learned how to defend ourselves from physical and psychological harm by fighting back, running away, sarcasm, over-performance, lying, and many others. We also developed patterns of thinking about ourselves, life, others and God that often were contrary to God's word...all the above is "flesh" (living, reacting in life out of my former resources).

FLESH IS ALSO DESCRIBED AS HOW WE MAKE LIFE WORK TO MEET OUR NEEDS

There are many influences in life that assist in the development of your unique flesh such as birth order, parents, siblings, peers, significant events, trauma, rejection, school, church, culture, tradition, et. al. Your exclusive flesh can manifest itself in many types of behavior both negative and positive...either way, it's still flesh. A further definition of flesh from my perspective might be,

habits or patterns of thinking, emoting and behaving often entrenched over time to fulfill a need/drive/passion/desire, or respond in a relationship, that is contrary to Christ and His grace.

Let me offer one more word about our physical body. Can our physical body actually tempt us? Normally, our physical body simply expresses physical needs and our thinking and emotions interpret/investigate ways to fulfill them (again, where most temptation begins); lust would be longing to fulfill them outside of Christ and His word...a pattern of thinking or behaving out of lust could be described as flesh.

In some cases, however, the body itself can entice you to sin. Have you ever developed a "taste" for something where your body craves something very specific that "tempts" you to fulfill? These bodily cravings that you have indulged over the years can yet tempt you still...kinda like muscle memory.

Further, when chemical imbalances exist in the body that create physiological drives/desires that demand fulfillment outside of Christ and the boundaries of His word, you have a physiological enticement to sin. In some cases you may need to seek medical treatment to normalize the body so you can make effective choices to follow Christ by faith (there are many extremely smart medical professionals who can help here...don't be afraid to get medical help when your body seems to be working against you).

YOUR BODY IS NOT EVIL, IT IS A MEANS BY WHICH WE EXPRESS OURSELVES IN THIS WORLD

Let me be clear...your body is not evil nor are legitimate physical desires, they are simply God given needs; the body, however, can entice when it is out of balance chemically (hormone imbalance, drugs, alcohol, et. al) and/or has developed bodily "cravings" that demand a fleshly fulfillment. These issues do NOT make you less of a Christian, they simply exist and should be dealt with properly and with grace.

Jesus was tempted by Satan to turn a rock into bread capitalizing on His natural but intense hunger at the moment. He was also tempted to defend His identity outside of the Father's plan, baited with power and prestige and later lured to turn away from the Father's redemptive plan by a close friend already deceived by the enemy (Matthew 4:1-11; 16:21-23). Legitimate needs, drives and passions were attacked and used against Jesus to sin, but the enemy failed.

60

When does hunger (a legitimate need) turn into temptation…when we desire to fulfill that need outside of Christ and His plan. When does intimacy or sexual fulfillment become temptation…when we desire and attempt to meet that need outside of Christ and His plan. When does advising a close friend to avoid certain death as Peter did become a tool of the enemy…when we think we can accomplish our purpose outside of Christ and His plan.

I see five basic categories of this word "flesh" as used in scripture, I call it B5; all are referred as "flesh" in scripture thus context, context, context is so important:

B5

1. **B**ehavior apart from Christ
2. **B**eing, self, or nature
3. **B**eliefs or mindset
4. **B**ackground & Bloodline
5. **B**ody or physical characteristics

1. Behavior apart from Christ
"Now the deeds of the flesh are evident, which are: immorality, impurity, sensuality,…." -Galatians 5:19

"Those who desire to make a good showing in the flesh try to compel you to be circumcised, simply so that they will not be persecuted for the cross of Christ." -Galatians 6:12

2. Being, self or nature
"Now those who belong to Christ Jesus have crucified the flesh with its passions and desires." -Galatians 5:24

"For we know that our old self was crucified with him so that the body ruled by sin might be done away with, that we should no longer be slaves to sin" -Romans 6:6 NIV

"Among them we too all formerly lived in the lusts of our flesh, indulging the desires of the flesh and of the mind, and were by nature children of wrath, even as the rest." -Ephesians 2:3

"For the mind set on the flesh is death, but the mind set on the Spirit is life and peace, because the mind set on the flesh is hostile toward God; for it does not subject itself to the law of God, for it is not even able to do so, and those who are in the flesh cannot please God. However, you are not in the flesh but in the Spirit, if indeed the Spirit of God dwells in you. But if anyone does not have the Spirit of Christ, he does not belong to Him." -Romans 8:6–9

"and in Him you were also circumcised with a circumcision made without hands, in the removal of the body of the flesh by the circumcision of Christ. -Colossians 2:11

3. Beliefs or mindset

"For even when we came into Macedonia our flesh had no rest, but we were afflicted on every side: conflicts without, fears within." -2 Corinthians 7:5

"For the mind set on the flesh is death, but the mind set on the Spirit is life and peace, because the mind set on the flesh is hostile toward God; for it does not subject itself to the law of God, for it is not even able to do so, and those who are in the flesh cannot please God." -Romans 8:6–8

4. Background & Bloodline

"Since many boast according to the flesh, I will boast also. ... Are they Hebrews? So am I. Are they Israelites? So am I. Are they descendants of Abraham? So am I. Are they servants of Christ? — I speak as if insane — I more so; in far more labors, in far more imprisonments, beaten times without number, often in danger of death...." -2 Corinthians 11:18-28

"What then shall we say that Abraham, our forefather according to the flesh, has found?" -Romans 4:1

"That is, it is not the children of the flesh who are children of God, but the children of the promise are regarded as descendants." -Romans 9:8

5. Body or physical characteristics
"All flesh is not the same flesh, but there is one flesh of men, and another flesh of beasts, and another flesh of birds, and another of fish." -1 Corinthians 15:39

"For we who live are constantly being delivered over to death for Jesus' sake, so that the life of Jesus also may be manifested in our mortal flesh." -2 Corinthians 4:11

"for no one ever hated his own flesh, but nourishes and cherishes it, just as Christ also does the church," -Ephesians 5:29

Never forget that you are already victorious "in Christ", BUT that fact does not shield you from temptation. You live in a physical body on this earth and the enemy of your soul would love nothing better than to see you falter and fail in your Christian experience.

So what's next in this process of temptation? Let's examine what happens when unchecked lust or flesh that takes us down an inevitable road of failure and defeat.

"when lust has conceived, it gives birth to sin"

At what point are we tempted according to James 1:14? Describe the word pictures used by James.

Define the idea of "flesh" with respect to your old or former self?

Describe the idea of your "own lust"? What is the driving force behind lust?

What are some struggles you face with your unique flesh?

6

It's a Baby!

Conception

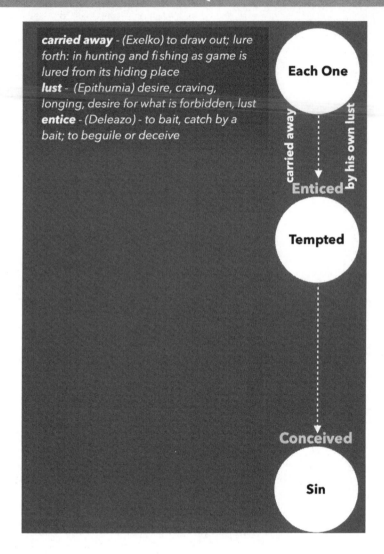

carried away - *(Exelko) to draw out; lure forth: in hunting and fishing as game is lured from its hiding place*
lust - *(Epithumia) desire, craving, longing, desire for what is forbidden, lust*
entice - *(Deleazo) - to bait, catch by a bait; to beguile or deceive*

Each One

carried away

by his own lust

Enticed

Tempted

Conceived

Sin

When does life begin?

What a powerful question. Answering that one question drives so many other beliefs. Did you know that sin has a life of its own, in fact, "when lust has conceived it brings forth sin". The word "conceive" means to catch or apprehend and hold on; it can also refer to conception in the womb. Have you thought about the process of conception? Once an egg is released it moves into the fallopian tube where it stays for about 24 hours waiting for a single sperm to fertilize it. Incredible...and billions of people later, the process still works just fine. Likewise, it will come as no surprise that the process is still alive and well with respect to our failure and sin. Once we are lured away and hold on to the lie of the enemy (he is the father of all lies), embracing it as our own (as true and necessary to meet whatever need is in play at the moment), it brings forth sin. Sin is often conceived with a thought we accept and grows in the womb of our mind until it is birthed to the outside world in our behavior. Countless sins later, we can confirm the process works as described.

"SINNING" DOES NOT MAKE YOU A "SINNER" ANY MORE THAN SWIMMING MAKES YOU A FISH

Although the process is in play every day of our lives, we are often simply unaware. Awareness is ground zero to experiencing victory, and the one who understands this process is a step ahead in experiencing God's victory! The enemy of our souls will attack this very foundation deceiving you in thinking that YOU are the problem, that YOU are defective and that Christ is NOT enough, especially for someone like YOU. It's a lie people! The enemy wants you to believe that sin is just a part of who you are and of course you sin, I mean, you are by nature a sinner...right?

Don't fall for the bait and switch. "Sinning" does not make you a "sinner" any more than swimming makes you a fish. You have an essential spiritual nature that is either alive in Christ or dead in Adam, either light or darkness, forgiven or unforgiven, holy or unholy, saint or sinner...which one are you?

This idea of conception is critical. We all have human desires for love, acceptance, fulfillment, success, recognition, value, security, safety, peace, and more. You desire love and are enticed to seek out an illicit physical expression. You crave acceptance and are deceived that going along with the crowd will do it for you. Why can't you be successful like everyone else? You believe the lie that cheating or cutting corners will give you the edge. You are scared and need security so naturally you can't break away from what you know is a bad situation, right?

We all at times grab hold of the promise (the "lie") to fulfill these desires outside of God's design as something that is true (at least in the moment) and the baby of sin is conceived, and as it grows it is nothing more than the personification of death.

Conception can lead to a quick birth or could gestate over time and finally give birth. You might actually give birth to twins or triplets! Perhaps you birth a private sin and then a sin of angry words against family or friend and then perhaps a sin of pride in denying all the above. So many babies!

Unfortunately, we see all the babies and start to accessorize with new baby clothes trying to dress up our sin baby to look so adorable and cute. As the baby grows we naturally need a stroller (or for those hard core parents, a running stroller) to carry the load of this heavy baby as we go about our daily routine. How are you accessorizing?

The old is gone

Have you ever thought to yourself, "I will never change" or "nothing has changed"? I hope you realize by now that simply is not true. You HAVE radically changed! OK, you still may make bad choices or suffer with crippling depression and anxiety but the truth is you are changed. I know…so what, it doesn't seem to be helping you at the moment, right? I get it. So did a guy named Paul who wrote over half the New Testament. This is NOT a new conversation, it is as old as the New Testament itself.

YOU HAVE RADICALLY CHANGED!

Paul was constantly reminding believers in Christ of their radical new identity and detailing what it looks like to walk in it. The problem is NOT whether or not the cross and resurrection actually worked, the issue is believing what we can not see (our preference is to see first then believe). Unfortunately I can not see the real me, the spiritual me, all I can see is my physical existence (nothing wrong with our physical existence, God is totally pleased with that part of me as well).

Your body has an incredible tool called a brain that has the ability to store vast amounts of information like a computer hard drive. Over time you and I have drawn conclusions about ourselves, life, God and others. We have experienced both positive and negative events; some of us have traumatic and unspeakable events in our life that have left their mark. All of these events, both real and even imaginary, are stored

69

in this incredible brain and shape how we view ourselves, life, God and others. Apart from the truth of God in Christ, this belief system is the foundation of our former self or "old self" thinking; it is unique to us and drives our own unique lust. Yes, the "old man" or "old self" or "old nature" is gone...dead...buried and replaced by our new self in Christ BUT the memories and old way of thinking are still alive and kicking! You are not crazy, we all have to deal with this stuff.

I know we already touched on this idea, but you and I are so comfortable operating out of the "flesh" (or former self) and it makes sense...we've been operating that way for a LONG time. We're used to it! It's familiar...it's what we know. The New Testament defines your former "self" as, *"slaves of sin"* (Romans 6:16, 20),

"And you were dead in your trespasses and sins in which you formerly walked according to the course of this world, according to the prince of the power of the air, of the spirit that is now working in the sons of disobedience" -Ephesians 2:1-2

You *"formerly lived in the lusts of [your] flesh, indulging the desires of the flesh and of the mind, and were by nature children of wrath, even as the rest"* -Ephesians 2:3;

"...you who were formerly far off" and without peace...a *"stranger and alien"* -Ephesians 2:13-19.

Are you still living like a "stranger and alien" with respect to Christ and His power in you? Do you accept the lies that you are *"far off"* from God, still a *"slave to sin"* and at your very core a sinner deserving of God's judgment? What are some of YOUR unique, false beliefs about yourself, life, God or others? These and many other "beliefs" are cataloged in that hard drive of a brain often operating at a near subconscious level; many are assumptions that you never question but MUST question if you are to experience His victory! These old beliefs, though false, tend to validate the lies from the enemy to keep you in bondage and defeat.

Remember that old definition for insanity, "doing the same thing, the same way expecting different results." Does that sound like you dealing with temptation? Are you doing the same old thing the same old way and expecting to experience victory? Let's change it up.

When dealing with the temptation and sin, the first shift in our thinking is realizing that temptation or sin is NOT you...stop identifying with it. Once you identify with the sin or temptation, defeat is a part of who you are (at least in your thinking). The truth is you are NOT defined by your temptation or sin. In fact, you probably focus on your temptation or sin way too much.

As a believer in Christ your sin is forgiven...past, present and yes even future. It was ALL on the cross, every bit of it. Stop dwelling on it. Yes, temptation will come but it does not define you. Remember, you are ALREADY victorious in Christ. With respect to your old self, please remember, your old self does not exist after receiving Christ. Do you believe it? Or better, will you believe it?

"How shall we who died to sin still live in it?" -Romans 6:2

"knowing this, that our old self was crucified with Him, in order that our body of sin might be done away with [rendered powerless], so that we would no longer be slaves to sin; for he who has died is freed from sin." -Romans 6:6–7

"For you have died and your life is hidden with Christ in God."
-Colossians 3:3

"and in Him you were also circumcised with a circumcision made without hands, in the removal of the body of the flesh by the circumcision of Christ;" -Colossians 2:11)

I love that verse, the actual living person ("body") of the flesh was REMOVED when you accepted Christ!

"Therefore if anyone is in Christ, he is a new creature; the old things passed away; behold, new things have come." -2 Corinthians 5:17

You HAVE CHANGED, YOU ARE DIFFERENT
THE OLD HAS GONE AND THE NEW HAS COME

We often sabotage our experience of victory by refusing to accept that "we died to sin" and are now "alive to God" all because our experience does not align with the truth. At some point we must understand that our experience of the victorious truth in Christ does not make it true...it is true regardless of our experience. Do not try and readjust scripture based on your experience. The fact that you do not feel dead to sin or act dead to sin in no way means you are not dead to sin, it simply means you are not feeling or acting dead to sin. The fact that you commit a sin does not negate the truth that you are free from sin. Likewise, the fact that you act righteous does not make you righteous; you are righteous because of Christ and your righteous acts flow from that truth.

When you sin, you are believing an old lie you have come

to accept as true for you or believing a new lie from the enemy to fulfill you apart from Christ. You are free from the shackles or chains of sin, but once in a while you put them back on because they are familiar or just look cool, or so you think.

As our own unique flesh, the remnants of our former self, entices us to live and respond apart from Christ, I believe there are two major external tempters as defined in Scripture and highlighted in the middle of the diagram that add fuel to the fire of our own flesh...(1) Satan and (2) his world system. These tempters try to fool us into thinking the chains were never broken and that we are hopelessly and forever doomed to a life of despair and defeat OR attempt to reinforce a "self-made man" religion that nullifies the power of Christ in our life. Although the tempters are external to our life, their inside contact (our old flesh patterns and way of thinking) provides ample insider information and opportunity to further seduce you and I to sin.

"But how", you might ask? Can Satan read our minds? Of course not, but he and his evil host know you and I so well he can anticipate our almost every move (maybe you have a family member, spouse or significant other who does the same thing and no, I am NOT equating them with Satan!).

As a believer there is no need to fear Satan or the world system but it would be foolish to ignore his game plan to paralyze your walk with Christ! The tempters will find ways to trap us in our old way of thinking and believing, pushing the lie that our former self is still alive and well and the new self? Well, according to the tempters, "the new self is just wishful thinking", "it is something to work for but never really achieve", "it is a dream within a dream" (you know this one Princess Bride movie fans). The snipers are ready, are you?

Questions

Describe the idea of "conception" in the context of temptation.

How does the New Testament describe your former self?

Why are you so different after receiving Christ as Savior?

How do you tend to see yourself? Why?

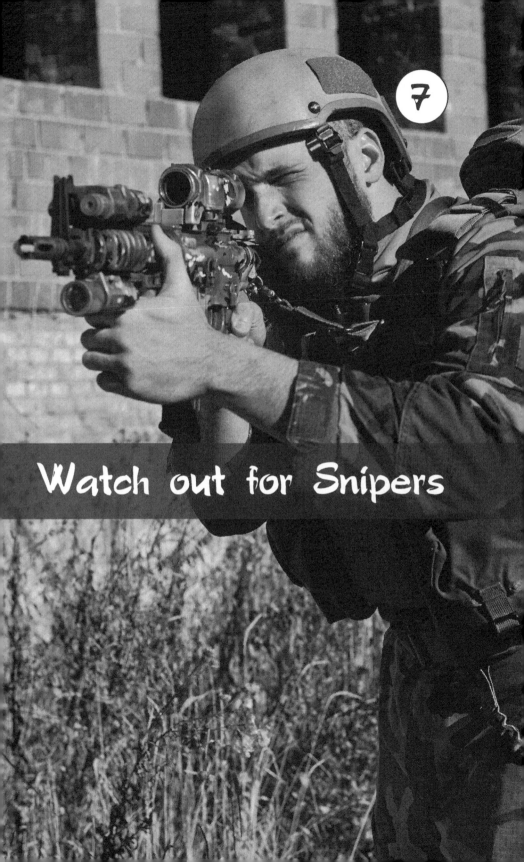

7

Watch out for Snipers

Who keeps messing with me?

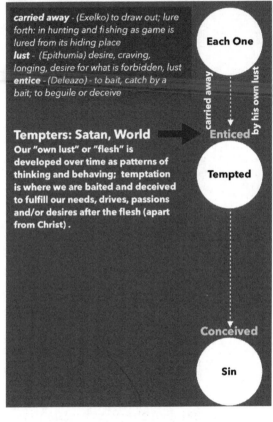

carried away - (Exelko) to draw out; lure forth: in hunting and fishing as game is lured from its hiding place
lust - (Epithumia) desire, craving, longing, desire for what is forbidden, lust
entice - (Deleazo) - to bait, catch by a bait; to beguile or deceive

Tempters: Satan, World
Our "own lust" or "flesh" is developed over time as patterns of thinking and behaving; temptation is where we are baited and deceived to fulfill our needs, drives, passions and/or desires after the flesh (apart from Christ).

Each One

carried away

by his own lust

Enticed

Tempted

Conceived

Sin

Satan - The Evil One

Satan is often characterized as a mysterious evil force or an evil supreme being on par with God…nothing could be further from the truth in my understanding. He is extremely powerful as compared to humanity but doesn't even rate on the scale when compared to God. As best I can gather from scripture, Satan is a singular angelic being who chose against God persuading 1/3 of the angelic host to follow his doomed example…we know them as "demons" (described symbolically in Revelation 12:4). These demonic forces are looking to deceive and destroy your walk with Christ in any and every way using both "positive" and "negative" strategies to achieve their goal.

Positive and negative? What's wrong with a positive influence? It does sound a bit crazy. I mean, we all want to be a positive influence on our kids, society, our friends, etc. so how could that be a tool of the enemy? In the context of our walk with Christ, Satan will not only attempt to trip us up with the usual temptation around obvious evil but often deceives us into doing good in our own strength and former fleshly resources…sometimes this temptation can be more devastating! We begin to believe and trust in our own strength and ability versus Christ and the cross…many, many believers get proud and haughty in what THEY are doing FOR God. I believe the enemy has won a great many battles here.

WATCH OUT FOR THE COMBINATION PUNCH!

If the enemy can get a "positive" foothold, he often continues for the one-two knock out punch with a good old solid immoral type temptation. He's basically got you trusting in your good behavior record where you are no match for his fiery missiles. The battle blueprint applies to both the positive and negative temptations, but more likely than naught, we apply it for the negative. If Satan can tempt you to sin after your great show of self-reliance and positive, good behaviors your emotional foundation is often cracked. He then pours on the condemnation for your "fall" even though he played both sides of the fence (building up your strength then exploiting your weakness).

Satan and his forces are master tempters; that's what they do 24/7. They try and distract us and "steal" God's word from our hearts so it doesn't take root. They disguise themselves in goodness and light to draw us away from the only source of true "goodness". They deceive us to believe a lie calling good evil and evil good. Satan has a portfolio of deceit customized just for you. He will use whatever it takes to unplug you from total dependence on Christ as your only source of power. Is Satan behind every temptation you face on a daily basis? Not exactly. He has engineered this world system in such a way that many times the world itself and the thinking patterns you've developed over the years tempt you without his direct intervention. Make no mistake, however, Satan is not absent from the scene but actively seeking how best to destroy all those who hold to the truth of Christ and His word.

Let's take a look at some New Testament scripture that provides a Biblical profile of the enemy:

- Matthew 4:1-11 - He tempts us
- Matthew 25:41 - Eternal fire is prepared for him
- Mark 4:15 / Luke 8:12 - He tries to steal and distract God's word from our mind
- Luke 22:31 - He is under the authority of God
- John 8:44 - He is a murderer and liar
- John 13:2 - He places thoughts in our minds
- 2 Corinthians 2:11 - He takes advantage of us through well-devised schemes
- 2 Corinthians 11:14 - He disguises himself in goodness and light
- 1 Thessalonians 2:18 - He hinders us in our journey
- 1 Timothy 3:6 - He fell because of his pride
- 1 Timothy 3:7 - He sets traps
- 1 Peter 5:8 - He seeks to devour us
- Revelation 2:10 - He can manipulate circumstances
- Revelation 12:12 - He has a short time on earth

So, how do you fight such an enemy? Hold on there just a minute, aren't you forgetting something? Yep, that's right...the war is over and Satan is a defeated foe. In Christ you have victory over the enemy no matter how loud and how often he chides you. I do not see where you and I are commanded to battle the enemy, we are simply told to "resist" under the authority of the Victor, Jesus Christ. And where do we resist? It starts in the mind where we make a decision to believe or not believe the truth that sets us free. Submitting to the truth, resisting the lies and choosing to walk free.

"Submit therefore to God. Resist the devil and he will flee from you." -James 4:7

"Put on the full armor of God, so that you will be able to stand firm against the schemes of the devil." -Ephesians 6:11

"It was for freedom that Christ set us free; therefore keep standing firm and do not be subject again to a yoke of slavery." -Galatians 5:1

The weight of the world

The World System

The world system is another external tempter; it is controlled by Satan and extremely effective at enticing us to sin. The "world" plays to our unique flesh patterns in an attempt to lure us away from our dependence on Christ.

Is the world bad? Should I go and live in a cave so the evil world does not rub off on me? There may be some called to isolation, but for most of us we're commanded to live in the world just not be corrupted by it. So, what is the world system?

"For all that is in the world, the lust of the flesh and the lust of the eyes and the boastful pride of life, is not from the Father, but is from the world." - 1 John 2:16

"The lust of the flesh and the lust of the eyes and the boastful pride of life" is how the scripture describes the world system in this struggle we all face. Let's take a look at each one.

The lust of the flesh

"The lust of the flesh" describes all the world has to offer that satisfies our physical and emotional appetites. Sensual, safety/security, emotional, physical and every other variation of fleshly need or desire…the world offers many alternatives to trusting God in these areas. For just about any physical need or desire you have there is a worldly solution just waiting for you. In some cases, these are classified as negative solutions…drugs, alcohol, illicit sex, adult entertainment, stealing, etc. The world, however, also offers positive solutions that tempt you to trust in yourself or the world as your very life, source and strength. Financial security, benefit plans, success strategies, etc. Again, there is not anything wrong with taking appropriate drugs for medical issues, but when we depend on them to "cope" we've fallen into the world's trap. What about financial security…IRAs, 401Ks, investment funds, stock portfolios, etc? Nothing at all wrong with those, but when our trust turns away from Christ to these financial instruments we've yielded to temptation. The "lust of the flesh" is the world's strategy to substitute fake pearls for the real "pearl of great price"…it is a strategy of worldly satisfaction.

The "World" plays to our unique flesh patterns

The lust of the eyes

"The lust of the eyes" is another description of the worldly system that entices us to sin through a focus and strategy of dissatisfaction. We are visual creatures. Proverbs 27:20 says that the eyes of man are never satisfied. We always want, and want more, and once we get it we are not satisfied and look yet again for something else to satisfy us. Remember as a kid getting that one toy you REALLY wanted only forgetting about it a few months, weeks or sometimes as few as days later? For my kids, I could buy them the coolest toy they were begging for only to find them begging for something else the next day. This worldly strategy attempts to deceive you into believing you are missing something or missing out whether it is a material item, relationship, position, finances, spirituality, appearance, or many other areas.

Have you ever analyzed your position in life (you know, against how others are doing)? Sometimes we look at where we think we should be or set goals to be where we think we want to be and low and behold, our complete focus is off of Christ. We have been deceived by the "lust of the eyes" dissatisfaction strategy.

Some believers are deceived in the spiritual arena…there is some "gift" they do not have or an experience they long for. What happens? Often, they spend their time, energy and focus on pursuing that gift or experience instead of resting in Christ and His grace. Pursuing a goal or a dream is not sinful; the temptation becomes apparent when we pursue that goal or dream apart from Christ and His word.

TEMPTATION DOES NOT EQUAL SIN

The boastful pride of life

The third installment of worldly enticement is the "boastful pride of life". This can work in concert with the other two very nicely. Here, the temptation is to claim victory or success by your own strength or what we also call your old, former resources or "flesh". You "pulled yourself up by your own bootstraps".

Perhaps you were trapped in a sin to satisfy your flesh. You set a course to clean-up your act and make your own path straight and you did it! Although your accomplishment is admirable it might actually be counterproductive; your success might reinforce some wrong thinking about the source of your new found morality boasting in your courage and tenacity to make it this far.

What might be a better approach? Once you realized your plight, the first step might be a total acknowledgment of your dependence on Christ, recognizing His forgiveness and thanking Him for the power and victory available in Christ. Interestingly, you might do some of the same activities as your life changes, but your motivation is quite different. One is depending on your ingenuity and strength while the other is depending on Christ. The "boastful pride of life" entices you to trust yourself, YOUR wisdom, YOUR finances, YOUR job security and more instead of Christ.

The world system is engineered by Satan to entice you to sin and interacts with your own unique flesh. If your unique flesh patterns tend to be negative, the negative influences in the world are ever present to entice you. If your flesh patterns and habits tend toward the positive, the world offers many ways to encourage your performance with strong positive reinforcements along the way. Pride encourages us to either hide our weakness or boast in our success. What an incredible system of enticement the enemy can wield against our faith. Satan deceives and uses this world system to entice us to sin. Remember, the enticement or temptation is not sin, it's how we respond that matters.

Questions

Describe how Satan might use a one-two or combination punch?

Provide some insight on Satan, who is he and how does he tempt us?

What are the three categories of the world system described in 1 John 2:16? Describe each category.

Describe a time when the enemy or the world tempted you.

8

The Battle is the Lord's

The thrill of victory

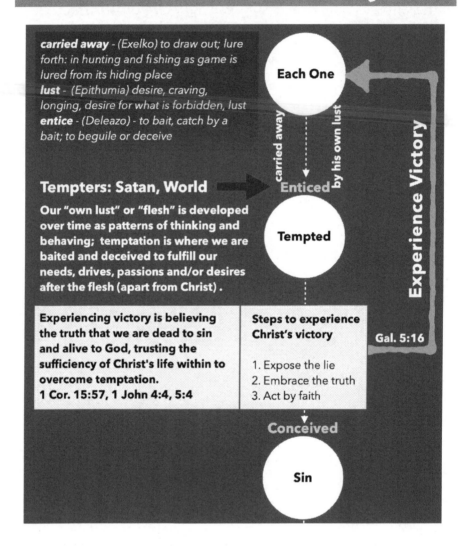

carried away - *(Exelko) to draw out; lure forth: in hunting and fishing as game is lured from its hiding place*
lust - *(Epithumia) desire, craving, longing, desire for what is forbidden, lust*
entice - *(Deleazo) - to bait, catch by a bait; to beguile or deceive*

Tempters: Satan, World

Our "own lust" or "flesh" is developed over time as patterns of thinking and behaving; temptation is where we are baited and deceived to fulfill our needs, drives, passions and/or desires after the flesh (apart from Christ).

Each One

carried away

by his own lust

Enticed

Tempted

Experience Victory

Experiencing victory is believing the truth that we are dead to sin and alive to God, trusting the sufficiency of Christ's life within to overcome temptation. **1 Cor. 15:57, 1 John 4:4, 5:4**	Steps to experience Christ's victory Gal. 5:16 1. Expose the lie 2. Embrace the truth 3. Act by faith

Conceived

Sin

Remember, temptation is NOT sin (review the diagram) but rather an opportunity for you to experience Christ and His victory in your life. Now, there's no need to seek out temptation to experience Christ...that's just plain dumb and to say the least, not God's plan.

Experiencing victory IS the normal Christian life and is not reserved for "super" Christians. Don't stop here just because you think YOU are different or your situation, background, environment is unique...of course it is and you are different from everyone else BUT the same omnipotent, loving God lives on the inside of you longing to express His Life in each and every situation including your temptations, struggles and strongholds.

EXPERIENCING VICTORY IS THE NORMAL CHRISTIAN LIFE

Experiencing victory goes something like this...you are tempted or enticed to sin by Satan or the world. The battle rages on many fronts to defeat you and cause sin to conceive as a result of this temptation. Instead of yielding to the temptation, you choose to believe and trust Christ as your victory and by God's grace experience the supernatural victory of Christ. As other temptations come, you apply the same process of trusting Christ and receiving His victory and thus the pattern begins where victory is a normal part of your life. Doesn't that sound so simple? Well, simple yes but easy...I don't think so. If it were easy, we wouldn't have so many Christians living in defeat and trying to figure all this stuff out.

Mike Quarles, author of many books including "Freedom From Addiction", and I hear one question over and over again as we explain these truths..."so tell me what to do, what steps do I need to follow"? Mike, in his southern, Alabama drawl, will generally say "there is nothing you can do"! Of course, that does not always sit well with the person asking, but Mike knows the question itself often reveals that a person has not yet understood the truth of their identity and union with Christ. However, in order to help those who prefer an outline or "steps" to consider, I offer the below as a guide.

Steps to experience Christ's victory

So, how do I experience His victory? The answer is to simply "believe". The Christian life is a life of faith and experiencing victory is no different. Many, however, find it difficult to grasp that concept so I have provided what I call the "Steps to experience Christ's victory". Please understand, the "steps" are NOT a magical formula but rather a process pointing you to Christ and supporting you in the decision to "believe". Christ lives in YOU and has already won the victory...our part is learning how to experience and rest in His victory. Understanding the enemy's strategy of deception points us to our first step:

1. Expose the lie

It's difficult if not impossible to experience victory if we accept as true the enemy's accusations, temptations, etc.

When faced with a temptation, examine your thinking at that moment...what are you believing about the temptation? Do you believe it will satisfy or fulfill you? Perhaps you believe at the moment you will gain in some way personally, professionally, socially, even spiritually! First things first... don't let the enemy sugar coat the temptation...call it like it is. "This is pornography", "this is gossip", "____ (fill in the blank) will not fulfill me" or "this is pride". You want a JOLT of reality (like a splash of cold water on your face) as you move to step 2.

2. Understand the need

Behind most every temptation is an unmet need fueling the fire. The need might be emotional, physical, social or spiritual. Sometimes a sexual temptation is not so much fueled by a physical need but an emotional or social one. If the deceiver can tempt us to accept that we are unloved, insecure, of no value, not satisfied, rejected, not safe, an outcast, and more he has a field day tempting us to fulfill those needs outside of Christ. Ask the question, "what need am I really trying to satisfy here?" You may not have the answer right away but asking the question will set you up for step 3.

3. Embrace the truth

Embrace the Truth. What truth? Well, how 'bout the truth of your identity. How 'bout the fact that you are dead to sin, alive to God, forgiven and free! How 'bout the fact that Christ IS your life and your victory right now! Perhaps you embrace the fact of God's abundant grace and love. You know that need you identified earlier…Philippians 4:19 says *"And my God will supply all your needs according to His riches in glory in Christ Jesus"*. Recognize that you are loved, accepted, valued, safe and poised to experience the peace of God right now. At this point, it is so very helpful to have God's word "hidden in your heart" through memorization and meditation. Often when the temptation hits, you don't have your Bible available so why not have His truth ready and available at a moment's notice. Psalm 119:11 KJV says *"thy word have I hid in mine heart that I might not sin against thee."*

4. Act by faith

Act by faith, trusting Christ's sufficiency to overcome. If you're depending on your cleverness, strength, personality or anything else to overcome in the struggle you've already lost! Even if you avoid the behavioral "sin" you did so outside of faith…we are saved by faith and we are to walk by faith. At this point we take action...we stop, run, close our mouth, turn back or any number of actions. The scripture is full of "actions" we can take by faith.

Sadly, many believers take the scriptural principles and commands to heart but leave the power of Christ behind; they attempt to exercise these actions in their own fleshly strength only to experience eventual defeat. On the other hand, some believers who embrace the "grace-life" appear to believe they have no part in experiencing victory and that is not true either. Our part is to choose "Life". Do not throw out the New Covenant commands and principles as a reaction to "law" or legalism but rather take action by faith trusting Him as your very Life.

I would estimate that 90% or more of the temptations you face are in (or begin in) the mind. As we've outlined earlier, you have embedded beliefs about God, life, yourself and others formed over time as well as habits of behaving that form your unique flesh. The first action you want to take will involve your thought patterns around your identity and relationship to sin.

Verse	Identity	Relationship to sin	Verse
2 Cor. 5:17	New Creation	Free From Sin	Rom. 6:7
Eph.1:1	Saint	Sin shall not rule over me	Rom. 6:14
Eph. 4:24	Righteous and holy	Forgiven	Col. 1:14

If you feel the temptation is of a physical nature, scripture provides some additional actions for you to take by faith "in Christ". If you perceive a specific, demonic overtone to the temptation you can respond accordingly. If the "world" or "world system" is tempting you to sin, there are again targeted actions to address the deception. These commands and principles are not suggestions but rather God given responses to your unique situation.

Actions alone are hollow; actions in faith, knowing who you REALLY are in Christ and trusting Christ in you as your victory and life, are where the journey to overcome is realized.

Tempter / Flesh	Action	Verse
Thoughts	Capture your wayward thoughts Renew your mind in the truth Set your mind on things above	2 Corinthians 10:5 Romans 12:1-2 Colossians 3:1-2
Physical Body	Present your body to God for His use Make no provision for the flesh Flee lust and follow after righteousness	Romans 6:12-14 Romans 13:14 2 Timothy 2:22
Satan	Resist (stand against) Quote the scripture	1 Peter 5:9 Matthew 4:2-11
World	Deny (refuse or reject) ungodliness Say no to those who lead you astray Stop lying, speak truth; stop stealing, go to work and give; choose to build up not tear down others, and more.	Titus 2:12 Proverbs 1:10 Ephesians 4:25-32

For each action, the key point is that we trust Christ and his grace to act through us. 1 John 5:4 emphasizes the point: *"and this is the victory that has overcome the world--our faith"*. It is a supernatural transaction. I can't begin to tell you how many times I've experienced this in my life (I've crashed and burned and failed as well but let's talk about happy things at the moment).

I remember struggling in one area and attempting to fight a temptation with my own reasoning ability. After struggling for 10 or 15 minutes I then took my own advice (steps to victory 1-4)…it was very odd. There was no struggle (although I felt the "pressure" of the temptation I had ceased in my struggle). I began walking away (ACTION) trusting Christ as my sufficiency and strength…the victory can only be described as supernatural and that is what I desire for you, experiencing the supernatural life of Christ. There is one last step, and I think an important one.

5. Affirm God's grace

This step is an affirmation of our total dependence on Christ...it is the final nail in the coffin for that unique temptation at that specific time. Affirming God's grace declares that the "victory" was and is by His power and not my former fleshly resources or strength. You simply take a moment to reflect on experiencing His victory and offer your praise and thanksgiving for His supernatural grace.

"And God is able to make all grace abound to you, so that always having all sufficiency in everything, you may have an abundance for every good deed." -2 Corinthians 9:8

"And He has said to me, 'My grace is sufficient for you, for power is perfected in weakness.' Most gladly, therefore, I will rather boast about my weaknesses, so that the power of Christ may dwell in me." -2 Corinthians 12:9

"Therefore let us draw near with confidence to the throne of grace, so that we may receive mercy and find grace to help in time of need." -Hebrews 4:16

Remember, it's easy to get the cart before the horse (or in today's language, the trailer before the truck) as many Christians do; they focus on the ACTIONS like renewing their mind, saying no to the world, making no provision for the flesh and more in their own strength to "achieve" victory. **I can not emphasize this enough...Christ already won the victory at the cross, our job is to "rest" in His victory, not try to replicate it.** The ACTIONS are simply a response by faith trusting Him as our Source. The ACTIONS are NOT the victory, Christ is our Victory. So what does that look like? Here's a few examples.

"Thank you Lord that You are my Life; I trust you right now. These thoughts I'm experiencing are not from You. In Christ you made me holy and righteous and that is what I am"

"Father thank you that I do not have to yield to this temptation. I am a brand new creation in Christ; I am dead to sin and alive to God. This is not who I am...I'm choosing your path and walking in it right now."

"In Jesus strong name I resist Satan; I stand firm in your grace and trust Christ as my strength and redeemer. I believe and trust His word which says..."

What happens next?

I guess we're home free at this point...right? I wish that were true. The struggles we face are on so many fronts and our enemy is relentless in his quest to hinder our growth, BUT God's grace is always greater. Experiencing victory can be your normal experience; don't be deceived by the enemy! But what if you do fail in that moment?

The agony of defeat

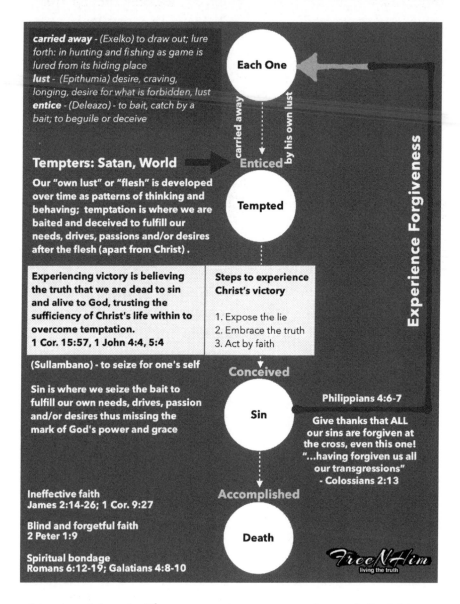

carried away - (Exelko) to draw out; lure forth: in hunting and fishing as game is lured from its hiding place
lust - (Epithumia) desire, craving, longing, desire for what is forbidden, lust
entice - (Deleazo) - to bait, catch by a bait; to beguile or deceive

Each One

carried away

by his own lust

Enticed

Tempters: Satan, World ➡️

Our "own lust" or "flesh" is developed over time as patterns of thinking and behaving; temptation is where we are baited and deceived to fulfill our needs, drives, passions and/or desires after the flesh (apart from Christ).

Tempted

Experiencing victory is believing the truth that we are dead to sin and alive to God, trusting the sufficiency of Christ's life within to overcome temptation.
1 Cor. 15:57, 1 John 4:4, 5:4

Steps to experience Christ's victory

1. Expose the lie
2. Embrace the truth
3. Act by faith

(Sullambano) - to seize for one's self

Sin is where we seize the bait to fulfill our own needs, drives, passion and/or desires thus missing the mark of God's power and grace

Conceived

Sin

Philippians 4:6-7

Give thanks that ALL our sins are forgiven at the cross, even this one!
"...having forgiven us all our transgressions"
- Colossians 2:13

Ineffective faith
James 2:14-26; 1 Cor. 9:27

Accomplished

Blind and forgetful faith
2 Peter 1:9

Death

Spiritual bondage
Romans 6:12-19; Galatians 4:8-10

Experience Forgiveness

FreeNHim
living the truth

You just blew it. The temptation came and you failed. You yielded to temptation and sinned. You seized the bait offered by the tempters to fulfill your own need, drive, passion and/

or desires in your own way thus missing the mark of God's power and grace. You feel awful. In many cases, this is not unfamiliar territory…you've been here before. You may feel sorrow, guilt, shame, a sense of loss, futility, anger and more. That's normal.

GRACE IS NOT EASY, IT COST CHRIST EVERYTHING

Confession or thanksgiving?

In the diagram you'll notice the one and only solution for a believer who has sinned…prayer with thanksgiving. What?

"Be anxious for nothing, but in everything by prayer and supplication with thanksgiving let your requests be made known to God. And the peace of God, which surpasses all comprehension, will guard your hearts and your minds in Christ Jesus."
- Philippians 4:6-7

That's right…when you blow it you are worried, anxious, upset and many other emotions (maybe not immediately but soon enough). Right then, at that exact moment, pray and thank God for His forgiveness and ask Him to help you understand even more of His grace and love for you. Sounds like an easy out? Not really…it cost Christ everything on your behalf!

So what about confession? I know, I used to think we should confess to receive God's forgiveness but wait a minute, ALL OUR SIN was forgiven on the cross! Why ask God to forgive what has already been forgiven? Remember, God chose to "remember our sin no more" and threw our sin away "as far as the east is from the west". You are already forgiven. Acknowledge your sin…absolutely (don't sweep it under the rug) but forgiveness was settled at the cross so thank God for it!

I know what you're thinking (and I used this same verse for years)...what about 1 John 1:9?

"If we confess our sins, He is faithful and righteous to forgive us our sins and to cleanse us from all unrighteousness." -1 John 1:9

My one question...when were you forgiven and cleansed from all unrighteous? That's right, when you believed and accepted Christ as your Savior. Do you need to be cleansed again? I don't think so.

As I dive into this chapter, I see John writing to a mixed audience of his brethren the Jews (don't make the mistake of thinking "brethren" means fellow believer in every New Testament letter). In the first few verses of chapter 1 he shares some of his credentials (and those of his fellow workers). Basically, he was with Jesus...first hand, eye witness, no middle-man. After stating his credentials, He begins his "message" or letter in verse 5 (obviously to folks who have a misunderstanding about God).

John wants this audience to know Jesus and have a relationship with Him. In fact, in verse 2 he states his purpose "proclaiming" to them eternal life and desires in verse 3 they all enjoy true fellowship with the Father. Sounds like the start of a gospel message. When you finally get to verse 9, John uses the very familiar concept of confession to his Jewish audience.

Let me ask you a questions...when you "confess" to anyone, what are you looking for? That's right, forgiveness! John's Jewish audience understood the concept of and requirements for forgiveness...a blood sacrifice and in this case, the ultimate sacrifice of the perfect Lamb of God (Jesus) on the cross.

The word confess is the word *homologeo* meaning to say the same thing as another, i.e. to agree with, assent. Confession here is agreement with God about the nature of and remedy for our sin. He told the whole group, which included unbelievers, to simply believe and express to God 1 John 1:9 so they too could experience forgiveness and cleansing from ALL unrighteousness.

"I am a sinner and I need your forgiveness offered through Christ"

STOP BEGGING GOD FOR WHAT YOU ALREADY HAVE IN CHRIST... FORGIVENESS

Breaking news - this passage of scripture is NOT directed to the believer in Christ. Confession of sin to God seeking His forgiveness is NOT for the believer. Why? You are already forgiven in Christ.

Confession to others when we sin against them is absolutely appropriate, but you will not find in the New Testament, unless I just missed it, any requirement for believers, or those "in Christ", to confess to God for more forgiveness than what Christ already accomplished through the cross (unless He missed something). Look around all over the New Testament...I don't think it's there.

Now, I am NOT saying that a believer should never acknowledge their failure to God; of course we should come to God with EVERYTHING on our heart and mind and ask Him to reveal His grace, love, and acceptance even in the midst of our failure.

"Be anxious for nothing, but in everything by prayer and supplication with thanksgiving let your requests be made known to God. And the peace of God, which surpasses all comprehension, will guard your hearts and your minds in Christ Jesus."
- Philippians 4:6–7

Remember what Jesus said to the woman caught in adultery after everyone walked away,

"Straightening up, Jesus said to her, 'Woman, where are they? Did no one condemn you?' She said, 'No one, Lord.' And Jesus said, 'I do not condemn you, either. Go. From now on sin no more.'" - John 8:10-11

After you blow it, thank God for His forgiveness and by God's grace, "sin no more". Don't weep and wail for hours, days or weeks at how you can't believe you did this again (that, by the way, is another deception of the enemy and expresses a lack of faith in the finished work on the cross); at the same time, don't sugar coat the issue. You sinned, it was wrong, it does not reflect the person you really are in Christ. If you need to make something right with others...do it. Now go, and sin no more.

Habitual sin

So what about this "cycle" of sin for the believer? What's going on? Can believers sin and sin and sin like there's no tomorrow? Well, look at your own history and answer that question for yourself. As you grow in Christ and your understanding of His incredible grace, this will become less and less of an issue. For some reading this book right now, it is a very real problem! You experience life and victory in some areas of your life, but that one relationship or one habit (or perhaps more) are extremely challenging.

The scripture provides specific, battle-tested strategies to experience victory over the flesh, Satan and the world as you walk by faith in the midst of temptation. Understanding who you are in Christ and becoming an effectual doer of the word through faith are vital to move from a cycle of sin to a cycle of victory. If you find yourself continually defeated, it may be an indicator of an "addiction" or spiritual bondage.

Spiritual bondage

What is spiritual bondage? Spiritual bondage can be defined as any area of life where a believer is "captured" and/or "entangled" in a particular sin, habit, or mindset with seemingly little hope of escape; we know what's right but seemingly can not do it. Most often, Satan has undue influence or "control". It is a state where we "feel" separated from the Life and power of Jesus Christ in our life (although the truth is that nothing *"will be able to separate us from the love of God, which is in Christ Jesus our Lord"* -Romans 8:39).

As a believer, you have been set free from Satan's power but can come under his influence and control if you allow him access directly (conscious choosing against God and His Word) or indirectly via a passive faith. Spiritual bondage can manifest in various addictive behaviors (positive and negative), emotional instability, paralyzing fears, suicidal thoughts, seemingly unbreakable habits, and so much more.

Let's first dispel one myth often found in the church… spiritual bondage does not make you less of a Christian, less "spiritual" or less loved by God. If you are struggling today, take hold of the fact that you are a loved, accepted, righteous believer in Christ who simply is not experiencing the freedom Christ has provided…remember, God is on your side here and longs for you to experience His power and grace! Look again at the diagram at the beginning of the chapter…do you see yourself tempted, struggling to experience victory then overcome in failure and defeat only to start all over again? This cycle of sin is NOT the normal Christian life, that's just another lie! You can experience His freedom.

Spiritual bondage could manifest due to the following (not exhaustive, but will give you an idea):

1.   Willful disobedience to God and His word. I'm not talking legalism here. There are clear commands and principles in God's word that if ignored give Satan an advantage in our life…one major area is unforgiveness toward others (Ephesians 4:26). When you choose to stay angry and not forgive you give the enemy a foothold in your life.

2.   Pride. When we begin to value our opinion, our efforts, our physical appearance, our possessions, our

position or status, our heritage, et. al. above God and others, we are living in a state of pride. Satan has a field day in the life of a man or woman overcome with pride.

3.   Deception. Probably the #1 issue why believers are trapped in spiritual bondage. We believe a lie (or lies) and are not standing on the truth, most often around our identity in Christ. Satan, the great deceiver, has convinced us we'll never experience victory, that we're just a sinner saved by grace, or that sin/confess is a normal part of Christian living, or "what do you expect, you're just human" or any number of half-truths and all out lies about God, yourself, life, and others. Understanding the "theology" of your forgiveness and identity in Christ is one thing; believing and embracing the truth as true for YOU is quite another and is the foundation for you to experience victory. You might want to reread the first chapter (or read it for the first time for those of you who skip around...you know who you are!

4.   Satanic practices. Ok, this is obvious or perhaps for some of you, not so obvious. Any occult practice, astrology, fortune telling, etc. can open the door to demonic activity in your life. Renounce it and receive God's grace and power. Don't mess around with this stuff, you're just asking for trouble.

Again, the above is not exhaustive but intended to point out some reasons why we get into this trap. When we think of spiritual bondage we normally jump right to the extreme...either addictive behavior or a believer foaming at the mouth (ok, I don't believe a Christian can be possessed, but they can sure act that way). Spiritual bondage can be a focused area of attack in one area of your life (with admittedly tons of consequential damage) where you just can't seem to break free or a life riddled with issues (and anything in between).

If you're experiencing spiritual bondage in any degree, the offer of freedom awaits you. You are not defined by the sum of your failures, you are defined and identified as a brand new creation through the cross of Jesus Christ.

Death

"and when sin is accomplished, it brings forth death"

The final result of sin is described as "death". Death is best defined as the absence of life just like darkness is the absence of light; it can be described as "separation" from life. Sin leads to death in many ways including our effectiveness in ministry and other spiritual pursuits or even our personal faith journey where we can, believe it or not, forget who we are and what Christ has done for us and in us.

But whoever does not have them is nearsighted and blind, forgetting that they have been cleansed from their past sins.
-2 Peter 1:9 NIV

Sin leading to death can describe the true nature of spiritual bondage i.e. the lack of Christ's life and power flowing freely in our life (we are "separated" from experiencing the very Life that dwells in our spirit but never separated from Christ and His love). I believe it can also refer to a death of conscience where we lose our sensitivity to God's moral values…we accept good as evil and evil as good; perhaps a death or break in our relationships, our business ventures, or even our personal freedom (jail or prison is a separation from freedom). Sin leading to death can impact almost any area, including our physical life.

This sounds pretty onerous. Aren't you glad, however, that God is a God that raises the dead! Not even death can thwart God's plan. You are NEVER too far gone because you can NEVER be separated from the One who loves you so.

If you feel you're one of the living dead, there's hope in Christ. He can raise you out of the death and bondage to experience the freedom of His grace. Every day, in fact, every moment can be a new beginning to experience His victory. I wrote a poem that I hope will encourage you in your journey to experience Christ.

Is this on the cross?
By Vernon Terrell

Is this on the cross? Does grace cover all?
My callous and willful, deliberate fall?
Choices that led down a path I knew well,
Forward I went knowing soon I could fail.

God's voice grew fainter each step of the way,
Ignoring His prompting and shunning His grace.
Deception took hold and emotions grew strong,
Emboldening the lies that led me along.

I was caught in a trap, I took hold of the bait;
Temptation had won and determined my fate.
So, is this on the cross? Does grace cover all?
My callous and willful, deliberate fall?

Yes, and yes and yes I proclaim,
Even this is covered through faith in His name!
This deliberate sin, as bad as it was,
Was nailed to the cross, an act of His love.

You can not out sin the grace of the Lord,
He's provided for this, and so much more.
So do we just sin? May it never be!
You're dead to that stuff, do not be deceived!

He wants you to walk as the person you are,
Holy and righteous in victory and love.
Now dust yourself off, thank God for His grace;
In the strength of the Lord take your next step of faith.

Questions

What can I do to get victory?

Describe the steps to experience Christ's victory.

What are some ACTIONS I can take by faith when facing the struggle of temptation? What is the danger of ACTION taking?

What is habitual sin and spiritual bondage and why do we get trapped?

What should my response be to my failure and sin? How can we encourage each other after we blow it?

9

Stop Fighting

Stand firm

Knowing all of this is one thing; doing something with all this understanding is quite another! So what do you do? Ah, there's that question again! Well, you learn to "stand firm". The enemy wants you to fight in order to win...that assumes the war is still going on and that winning is in question.

Let me assure you...the war is over, Jesus already won. It is true that sin still exists on this earth and that you will in fact still sin, but it is also true that ALL of that sin, past, present and future was dealt with at the cross. "It is finished" (John 19:30). Change your perspective.

YOU ARE NOT FIGHTING TO WIN BUT CHOOSING TO REST IN HIS VICTORY

Your mission, should you choose to accept it, seems impossible in this human existence! And apart from Christ it is impossible! Your mission is to "stand firm" by faith in the victory that is already yours in Christ. Man up! Woman up! Stand firm.

"Be on the alert, stand firm in the faith, act like men [or women], be strong." -1 Corinthians 16:13

You have the victory in Christ; it is a gift for all those who are in Christ. Don't be fooled by well meaning folks that want to give you more rules to follow to increase your chances of victory...it's a trap! Rules or "law" are like gasoline to the flame, adding fuel to the fire of sin. Don't fall for it, "law" IS the power of sin!

"The sting of death is sin, and the power of sin is the law; but thanks be to God, who gives us the victory through our Lord Jesus Christ." -1 Corinthians 15:56–57

Stand firm against what seems to be impossible odds. Stand firm when your thoughts are all over the place and you are tempted to justify what you know is unjustifiable. Stand firm when your emotions tell you to give up, give in, or run away and hide. Stand firm when your body is driving you against what you know is right. Stand firm when others are telling you that you need more than what Jesus has already provided at the cross.

"Not that we lord it over your faith, but are workers with you for your joy; for in your faith you are standing firm."
-2 Corinthians 1:24

*"It was for freedom that Christ set us free; therefore keep standing firm and do not be subject again to a yoke of slavery [the law]." *-Galatians 5:1

*"Through Silvanus, our faithful brother (for so I regard him), I have written to you briefly, exhorting and testifying that this is the true grace of God. Stand firm in it!" *-1 Peter 5:12

RULES WILL NEVER PUT OUT THE FLAME OF TEMPTATION ANY MORE THAN GASOLINE WILL PUT OUT A FIRE

Now a book on temptation would not be complete without a discussion of Ephesians 6:10-20. Some folks will take this so literal that every morning they "put on their armor", like dressing for work (or battle) every day! If that is you, go for it, just don't make it some kind of legalistic ritual! The point here is not suiting up to pick a fight, it's learning how to "stand"! No need to go out and find a temptation to fight...it is coming your way!

Now many incredible authors and writers have brilliantly dissected this passage and I encourage you to find your favorite teacher and review their insights. I will simply provide a bit of color from my own perspective that I hope will add some value to the discussion. Let's read the passage and then I will highlight a few items for your consideration.

"10 Finally, be strong in the Lord and in the strength of His might. 11 Put on the full armor of God, so that you will be able to stand firm against the schemes of the devil. 12 For our struggle is not against flesh and blood, but against the rulers, against the powers, against the world forces of this darkness, against the spiritual forces of wickedness in the heavenly places. 13 Therefore, take up the full armor of God, so that you will be able to resist in the evil day, and having done everything, to stand firm. 14 Stand firm therefore, HAVING GIRDED YOUR LOINS WITH TRUTH, and HAVING PUT ON THE BREASTPLATE OF RIGHTEOUSNESS, 15 and having shod YOUR FEET WITH THE PREPARATION OF THE GOSPEL OF PEACE; 16 in addition to all, taking up the shield of faith with which you will be able to extinguish all the flaming arrows of the evil one. 17 And take THE HELMET OF SALVATION, and the sword of the Spirit, which is the word of God.

18 With all prayer and petition pray at all times in the Spirit, and with this in view, be on the alert with all perseverance and petition for all the saints, 19 and pray on my behalf, that utterance may be given to me in the opening of my mouth, to make known with boldness the mystery of the gospel, 20 for which I am an ambassador in chains; that in proclaiming it I may speak boldly, as I ought to speak." -Ephesians 6:10–20

Generally speaking, most people want to be strong or accomplished in what they do. Paul encourages the Ephesians to be "strong in the Lord and in the strength of His might". You might envision a body builder, or mixed martial arts expert with a Bible in one hand ready to defend themselves and the faith, but I am not sure that is the right picture. I would like to focus here on whose strength we are talking about?

The word used is *"endunamoo"* combining the words *"en"* and *"dunamoo"*. The word *"en"*, as defined by "The NT Word

Study Dictionary" by Dr. Spiros Zodhiates, means "in, on, at, by any place or thing, with the primary idea of rest" and *"dunamoo"* means "to strengthen". It is not referring to you or I working out our spiritual muscles through some challenging Biblical or prayer exercise program. We choose to rest in the strength and power of the Lord Jesus Christ. Sometimes, like the apostle Paul, it looks like,

"Therefore I am well content with weaknesses, with insults, with distresses, with persecutions, with difficulties, for Christ's sake; for when I am weak, then I am strong." -2 Corinthians 12:10

WE ARE STRENGTHENED BY RESTING IN HIS STRENGTH, POWER AND ABILITY IN AND THROUGH US

The other words in Ephesians 6:10 are equally compelling. We are strengthened by His *"kratos"* ("power, force or dominion") and His *"ischus"* ("might, power, faculty, ability"); we rest in His strength, in His display of power and ability operating in us, through us and for us, even in the midst of the most challenging circumstances. It is often through weakness when we see God's power manifested most in our lives.

Verse 11 tells us to "put on" as you would put on clothing "the full armor of God". Again, I do not think the intent here is to create a morning ritual (although if your morning routine reminds you of His strength, go for it!), but rather to explain the fact that we have an enemy who is working against us in this life. Our only job is to stand firm against the enemy's "schemes" or *"methodeia"* ("craftiness"), a methodical, well planned attack.

Verse 12 tells us the real enemy is NOT "flesh and blood"... your spouse, mother-in-law, kids, boss, neighbor or any other "flesh and blood" person is NOT the enemy. The real enemy is spiritual in nature and because of that, we need the "full armor of God" (which we already have in Christ) but need to learn how to "take up", "resist" and "stand firm" as we are exhorted in verse 13.

To "take up" means to carry it with you so you have it when needed in that "evil day", the time when the enemy comes against you, to "resist" or "oppose" him and "stand firm" against him.

So the armor consists of "having girded your loins with truth"; the illustration is to wrap your lower back and hips with the garment of truth; the expression can mean "to be in readiness for anything" according to Dr. Spiros Zodhiates. It's possible you may need to undress the lies (they really don't fit very well anyway) and replace them with truth.

BE RIGHTEOUS AND DO RIGHTEOUS BECAUSE THAT IS WHO YOU ARE

So we are strengthened in His strength and adorned with His truth ready for anything. What truth? How about the truth of His love for you, His forgiveness, and your new identity in Him. How about the truth of His grace, your union with Him where nothing can ever separate you from His love.

"and you will know the truth, and the truth will make you free." -John 8:32

*"Jesus *said to him, "I am the way, and the truth, and the life; no one comes to the Father but through Me." -John 14:6*

It is interesting that "righteousness" is a separate garment from truth in this illustration of armor. Our righteousness in Christ is part of the truth but Paul calls it out specifically, but why? I can't be sure but perhaps our righteousness in Him is the one thing that is designed to protect, among other things, our heart...our brand new heart. A heart that is no longer wicked, hard and made of stone, but because of Christ is now kind, loving, giving, obedient, forgiving and so much more.

When the enemy strikes, in that evil day (which could be any day), our new loving heart is often the target of the enemy with accusations like "you will never change", "you are wicked to the core", "stop pretending to be good". The enemy knows that if we "lose heart", any hope of experiencing victory is lost. We must "put on" that breastplate of righteousness in full assurance that our righteousness is secure in Him...you have it right now believer, so put it on! Your righteousness does NOT depend on you or your behavior, it is the very righteousness of Jesus Christ given to you by His grace. This righteousness assures that you have radically changed and that you are holy, righteous and good at the core of your being.

You may be under assault while serving the less fortunate, or fired-upon when counseling a friend or even when spending time with your family. The lies coming at you are specific, targeted and often relentless. "I am such a hypocrite, I have no business serving" or "I must defend and protect myself so I don't look weak or like a failure in front of my family". Standard enemy tactics, lies couched in first person singular designed as covert weapons confusing the believer to accept the thoughts as their very own.

THE ENEMY IS CONSTANTLY STIRRING UP RELATIONAL TROUBLE TRYING TO DIVIDE AND CONQUER

Put on the breastplate of righteousness and serve without any hesitation; be honest and stop defending your reputation. Go and be righteous and do righteous because that is who you are.

The illustration continues with putting on your shoes with the "preparation of the gospel of peace". Although this could very well mean sharing the gospel of Christ which provides the ultimate peace in Him (and if the door opens to share, do it), I think there may be something else here. I think most of us struggle with pride, anxiety, depression, anger, reputation management, bitterness, despondency and so much more in the area of relationships. The enemy is constantly stirring up relational trouble trying to divide and conquer. It's time to put on those shoes with a *"hetoimasia"* (preparation or readiness) with the good news of peace. Make a decision to move toward peace in your relationships. You may need to humble yourself, put aside your reputation, stop defending, walk away...you get the idea.

The "shield of faith" in verse 16 is your front line defense against all the enemy fire. We don't see the real enemy with our physical eyes nor do we see our heavenly Father in that way. For that matter, we don't see our new heart and righteous nature either. Our shield is our faith in the One who sees the enemy fire, who sees the real you in the midst of the barrage of missiles and the One who has already won the battle. Our shield of faith is trusting we are loved and made holy, righteous, victorious and free. If we dropped our shield, took a hit and have fallen we pick-up that shield to protect us while we regroup. We are forgiven and can do all things through Him who strengthens us.

We complete the armor in verse 17 with "the helmet of salvation, and the sword of the Spirit, which is the word of God". The helmet protects your brain and your thinking! If the enemy can cause you to doubt or forget the fact of your salvation, your deliverance, your redemption or reconciliation, your security or forgiveness or eternal life, you are likely to suffer a spiritual concussion!

"For he who lacks these qualities is blind or short-sighted, having forgotten his purification from his former sins. Therefore, brethren, be all the more diligent to make certain about His calling and choosing you; for as long as you practice these things, you will never stumble;" -2 Peter 1:9–10

Finally, in Ephesians 6:18, Paul pleads with his readers to pray and petition God at all times, and with this in view he tells them to "wake up and be vigilant" or *"be on the alert"* to petition God on behalf of himself and others. The exhortation is to us as well. Pray. *"Pray at all times in the Spirit"*.

Now don't read "pray in the Spirit" in this verse as some mysterious, out-of-body prayer experience (although God can certainly provide each of us with all kinds of unique experiences). Prayer in the Spirit is how we are to pray *"at all times"*. Paul described it like this in Romans 8:26,

In the same way the Spirit also helps our weakness; for we do not know how to pray as we should, but the Spirit Himself intercedes for us with groanings too deep for words;

When we pray, we trust the Spirit of God in us to intercede for us for that which we are unable to express adequately in words. He knows our heart and knows the exact petition according to the will of God. What an incredible comfort. We need not worry if we "prayed right" or said the "right words", we can trust the Spirit in us every time we pray! So pray!

It's not about you

I have some good news (although for some it might be a bit disconcerting). Life is NOT about you; you and I are not the center of existence that everything else revolves around. Experiencing victory or crumbling in defeat does NOT in any way alter God's plan for you, your family or the universe at large. Yes, sin has consequences and your choices will most often affect others in your sphere of influence.

God's plan for you and those you love is wrapped up in the person of Jesus Christ regardless of the choices you make (and by the way, He already knows every single one of them…you might want to let that sink in). Knowing Him, experiencing His grace, love and forgiveness through thick and thin, good times and bad times, always and forever, is the plan. You are going to fail at times, it's part of being human. Don't fall into the trap of holding yourself to some unrealistic standard of behavioral perfection. Learn the art of walking by faith, getting up by faith (after you stumble and fall), sharing your victories and defeats by faith..a life of humility, grace, kindness and love.

LIFE IS MORE THAN AVOIDING SIN, IT IS LIVING!

Although I wrote this book to help you understand the process of temptation and how to experience His victory, please do not focus so much on avoiding sin or you will miss the whole point...LIFE! Life is more than avoiding sin, it's LIVING! Go out and LIVE…be YOU, the brand new you in Christ. The remade you with the brand new heart. Enjoy life…enjoy Christ…enjoy each other. Stop trying so hard to figure out ways to keep yourself pure or at peace…you ARE pure and He is your peace! Of course, recognize the battle when it comes but rise above it on eagle's wings (if you're battling in the trenches, chances are you still believe that victory is up to you…it's not).

If you feel pressure to do something to win the struggle of temptation when it comes your way, I have not explained the truth adequately so let me restate. There is nothing more for you to do…IT IS FINISHED! It's time to lay down the boxing gloves. All the "to-dos" I mentioned earlier are simply reminders that it is already done (unless you believe you can improve on what Jesus already did, then by all means, go for it). Seriously, Peter reminded his readers the same thing in 2 Peter 1:3-4 NIV (and yes, I know I've mentioned this verse before),

"His divine power has given us everything we need for a godly life through our knowledge of him who called us by his own glory and goodness. Through these he has given us his very great and precious promises, so that through them you may participate in the divine nature, having escaped the corruption in the world caused by evil desires."

THERE IS NOTHING MORE FOR YOU TO DO, "IT IS FINISHED"!

You have everything you need…right now. I know you don't always feel like you do, but that is where faith comes in knowing that the cross and resurrection accomplished more than you can physically see. You are a brand new creation, God knows it, the enemy knows it, the problem is you have yet to realize it but once you do, boy oh boy, look out. Humility will begin to express itself in love 'cause you have nothing more to prove; victory will begin to be the norm and life as you know it will fundamentally change. Why? Are you doing something different? Well, yes you are probably doing things different but that did not cause the change, realizing the truth and resting in His grace made all the difference.

"Therefore if anyone is in Christ, he is a new creature; the old things passed away; behold, new things have come."
  -2 Corinthians 5:17

If all your needs are met in Christ; if your value and worth were settled at the cross; if your security is resting in the omnipotent God; if your reputation is no longer an issue because His grace is always sufficient; if worry and doubt are replaced with faith and love can you see how the "power of Christ" works through even your weakness?

"And He has said to me, "My grace is sufficient for you, for power is perfected in weakness." Most gladly, therefore, I will rather boast about my weaknesses, so that the power of Christ may dwell in me." -2 Corinthians 12:9

"And my God will supply all your needs according to His riches in glory in Christ Jesus." -Philippians 4:19

When we can take a breath and move our life out of the center limelight and trust Christ as our very life the entire paradigm will shift. Jesus does NOT want to bless my idea of what my life should be nor does He need my commitment to make something happen. He wants me to rest and experience His Life. He has already given me every blessing in Christ. He is pleased with me and desires to love others through me and my unique gifts, talents, resources, and more.

"Come to me, all you who are weary and burdened, and I will give you rest. Take my yoke upon you and learn from me, for I am gentle and humble in heart, and you will find rest for your souls. For my yoke is easy and my burden is light."
  -Matthew 11:28-30 NIV

Questions

Describe your "mission" in the temptation struggle?

How are we to be "strong in the Lord" in Ephesians 6:10?

How do we "take up" and/or "put on" the full armor of God"? What does it look like for you?

What is a possible reason why "righteousness" is listed as a separate, "breastplate" garment?

List a few paradigm shifts you see from this chapter?

10

Start Living

Walking by faith

Do you find yourself consumed with your failure? Are you constantly looking for that next book, message, seminar, webinar, blog, podcast or anything that might provide that missing link to help you in your quest for peace and victory? Well, I hope you understand at this point that Jesus is your peace and victory. I want you to stop focusing on your failure or potential failure and start living! Your sin is off the table...there is no more discussion...the cross settled the issue forever. God is not judging or condemning you. "But wait", you might shout, "what about 2 Corinthians 5:10-11,

"For we must all appear before the judgment seat of Christ, so that each one may be recompensed for his deeds in the body, according to what he has done, whether good or bad.

Therefore, knowing the fear of the Lord, we persuade men, but we are made manifest to God; and I hope that we are made manifest also in your consciences."

Absolutely correct! We will ALL appear for the judgment seat of Christ to be recompensed for our deeds while on this earth, whether good or bad. Here is my question to you, what is another word for "bad" in the scripture? Did you guess it?

BAD = SIN

As a believer in Christ, what happened to your sin? That's right, it is forgiven, paid-for, all judgment for your sin fell on Christ at the cross; He took it all, buried it and gave you His righteousness. So when you stand at the judgment seat of Christ, what category are you in, "good or bad"? The awesome news is that you are "good". Stop reminding me of all the bad stuff you have done and have yet to do...the cross has you covered.

What about the "bad"? Well, apart from Christ, even all "good behavior" or "righteous acts" are like "filthy rags" (Isaiah 64:6 KJV). Remember what Jesus told the man who ran up to him in Mark 10:18,

"And Jesus said to him, "Why do you call Me good? No one is good except God alone."

Those who choose not to believe (those who choose not to receive the free offer of forgiveness and life) fall in the category of "bad" in this context. There are only two categories, "in Adam or in Christ", "in darkness or in light", "a child of wrath or child of God", "a sinner or a saint", "unforgiven or forgiven", "unrighteous or righteous", "in the flesh or in the Spirit". If you are in Adam, only judgment remains; if you are in Christ, there is no more judgment.

"He who believes in Him is not judged; he who does not believe has been judged already, because he has not believed in the name of the only begotten Son of God." - John 3:18

"Therefore there is now no condemnation for those who are in Christ Jesus." -Romans 8:1

Having said that, don't think that you and I can escape the consequences of our bad decisions on earth. Of course there are consequences to sin or bad choices, but don't think for a minute that God is punishing you when you blow it, that just isn't true. And don't believe the deception that says, "Oh, God is not punishing you, He is simply disciplining you when you sin". Seriously? Why would God "discipline" what He chooses not to remember any more? Using the word discipline in this context is just a fancy way of saying punish.

*"AND THEIR SINS AND THEIR LAWLESS DEEDS
I WILL REMEMBER NO MORE." - Hebrews 10:17*

Of course, God will use everything at His disposal to train us, guide us, disciple (discipline) and demonstrate His love for us, all for our good and His glory. Will He use pain and suffering that we experience in life? Absolutely. Is He causing the pain and suffering as a response to our "sin"... absolutely not!

So my message is...relax and start living your life right now! If you are in bondage to stuff that you just can't seem to break...get help! What are you waiting for? Take that next step of faith. If you have bad habits that are wreaking havoc on your peace and joy, take the insights learned in this book to break the cycle and start living, loving and serving now! Find someone or a group of someones that can encourage you in your journey (we are designed for relationship, don't go it alone if at all possible). Be humble, bring your issues to the light and stop hiding in the shadows. Live free, walk free, love free because you are free!

RELAX AND START LIVING

What does it look like?
Paul answers this very question in his letter to the church at Ephesus.

"So this I say, and affirm together with the Lord, that you walk no longer just as the Gentiles also walk" -Ephesians 4:17

My friend, you are no longer children of the darkness but are now children of the light; as Paul says earlier in the letter in Ephesians 2:19,

"So then you are no longer strangers and aliens, but you are fellow citizens with the saints, and are of God's household,"

Paul continues in Ephesians 4:22 on how to put feet to our faith.

"that, in reference to your former manner of life, you lay aside the old self, which is being corrupted in accordance with the lusts of deceit,"

The "old self" is a reference to your former way of living apart from Christ, i.e. the flesh. As we learned earlier, the flesh is composed of the lies and deception we believed about ourself, life, God and others and manifested through our attitude and behavior. We have a choice to "lay aside" these old patterns of thinking and behaving.

"and that you be renewed in the spirit of your mind,"
-Ephesians 4:23

As we lay aside the lies of our old belief system, we replace it with the truth of scripture to renovate our mind and thinking; understanding who we are in Christ, accepting the truth that God loves us...period. We are actually dead to sin and alive to God no matter how we feel, and so much more!

"and put on the new self, which in the likeness of God has been created in righteousness and holiness of the truth." -Ephesians 4:24

We then "put on" our new, righteous self. I know, that sounds weird. It's kinda like taking off an old coat and putting on a new one. Yes, we're talking behavior here. The old clothes (lying, unforgiveness, stealing, etc.) just don't fit right any more, but the new stuff, I'm telling you, fits just right.

Basically, walking by faith is walking as the new person you are in Christ. God made you holy, so walk holy. Why? It fits you! God made you righteous, so walk righteous. Your walking does not define or make you holy or righteous, it is simply an expression of the true you. Paul knows there will be questions so he provides some specific examples in Ephesians 4:25–26, 28-29,

"Therefore, laying aside falsehood, speak truth each one of you with his neighbor, for we are members of one another. Be angry and yet do not sin; do not let the sun go down on your anger"

"He who steals must steal no longer; but rather he must labor, performing with his own hands what is good, so that he will have something to share with one who has need. Let no unwholesome word proceed from your mouth, but only such a word as is good for edification according to the need of the moment, so that it will give grace to those who hear."

Many believers get this backwards and believe by doing righteous activities it will make them righteous; they are trying to earn or achieve what God has already given them. On the other hand, a few may misunderstand grace and not take a step of faith in the real world! As God teaches you His truth, allow Him to express His righteousness, victory, forgiveness and love through your decision to simply take that next step.

Final words

I hope this short book has been insightful and more than that, has impacted your journey to experience the love, grace and victory that is only found in Jesus Christ. You have so much to offer, don't short-change those in your sphere of influence that need to experience God's grace. Be the authentic, grace-filled, humble encourager who may not have his or her behavioral act 100% together but loves and serves nonetheless.

I created a little card that I sometimes hand out when I speak at the jail or other events. I joke about learning some new "F" words...don't judge me!

The idea here is that you will fail at times, and when you do make sure to "Fail, Forward", meaning that you don't wallow in your sorry and regret. Yes, you blew it and there may be consequences for your actions but get up, brush yourself off and move forward. One Christian author said the greater sin than the sin in question is remaining in your sorrow and regret essentially nullifying the grace and forgiveness of God.

"Faster". The longer you sit there and mull over your failure and hyper-analyze your defeat the greater chance the enemy will have to bombard you with thoughts of doubt and despair driving your feelings in a tailspin. Get over it. Yeah, I said it. As we said in an earlier chapter, if you hurt someone and need to make it right, make it right! If it is a private matter between you and you, sure, take a moment to grieve but make it quick please. That failure does not define you nor call into question that truth of who you are in Christ.

The next part of this statement says "walking in His Forgiveness and Freedom". That's right, get up and start walking in His forgiveness and freedom. Acknowledge your sin, absolutely, no need to try and deceive yourself but thank God for His forgiveness, thank God that even this has no power over you. You are free and victorious (you just did not experience that victory in that moment). Start walking. The enemy wants to immobilize you, don't let him. What needs to be done? Who needs a word of encouragement? Who can you love or serve? Praise God in song, read His word, encourage yourself in Him!

But why the last part, "by faith"? Because right now you definitely are not feeling very forgiven or free, are you? So you start walking by faith, in the midst of your anger (at yourself most likely), thanking God for His forgiveness, forgiving yourself and walking free. Don't look behind, keep moving forward. I understand learning from your mistakes, that's wisdom, but when you keep looking back you tend to miss what is just ahead.

On the flip side of this card it has a saying I came up with a while back.

"Until the reality within YOU is real, the real will never be YOUR reality"

-Vernon Terrell

...if anyone is in Christ, he is a new creation.
2 Corinthians 5:17

I can not make you believe the truth of your new identity in Christ. If I can convince you with my incredible arguments, such as they are, that you are a brand new creation who is dead to sin and alive to God, someone else, who perhaps is a bit more persuasive, can change your mind. You need to be fully convinced for yourself.

The "reality within you" is the truth of the brand new you in union with the omnipotent God in the person of the Holy

Spirit, "Christ in you the hope of glory", living in you right now.

The next idea in this statement says "is real". Is that truth I just mentioned "real" for you? Do you believe it? Do you know it? Is it simply a lofty idea but not a factual reality? Are you dead to sin? Are you a brand new creation? Is all of that true for YOU?

RELAX...REFOCUS...GIVE YOURSELF A BREAK!

Well, until you are convinced that the reality of Christ in you and you in Him is really real, the real will never be your reality (in your experience). Although the power is there, His Life is present, you are overflowing with His grace, love, forgiveness and victory, your unbelief will not allow you to access any of it. You may try and fake it, recite your identity verses, or quote your scripture out loud until the cows come home or Jesus returns, but none of that will have much effect.

BUT relax...it is all part of the journey. Really, give yourself a break (God certainly did). I want you to learn the value of rest. Stop forcing yourself, expecting more of yourself, deriding yourself, and just rest. Refocus your attention on receiving His love, basking in His grace, finding joy in the midst of the chaos (sometimes you do have to look harder on that one), thanking Him for His forgiveness, declaring the truth in spite of your current situation, sharing His grace, sharing His love, sharing His forgiveness and over time you may find those failures diminish and His victory just another day in what is now your typical life.

You have stopped fighting and started living.

Questions

What happens when we all appear before the Judgment Seat of Christ in 2 Corinthians 5:10? What about all the "bad" stuff?

What illustration does Paul use in reference to the old stuff and what is our response?

What spoke to you personally from this chapter and this book?

Made in the USA
Columbia, SC
23 December 2019